RSPB

Nature Guide

Mike Unwin

A & C Black • London

Published 2009 by
A & C Black Publishers Ltd.
36 Soho Square, London, W1D 3QY
www.acblack.com

ISBN 978-1-4081-0514-6

Text copyright © 2009 Mike Unwin

The right of Mike Unwin to be identified as the author of this work has been asserted by him in accordance with the Copyrights, Designs and Patents Act 1988.

A CIP catalogue for this book is available from the British Library.

All the internet addresses given in this book were correct at the time of going to press. The author and publishers regret any inconvenience caused if addresses have changed or sites have ceased to exist, but cannot accept any responsibility for any such changes.

This book is produced using paper that is made from wood grown in managed, sustainable forests. It is natural, renewable and recyclable. The logging and manufacturing processes conform to the environmental regulations of the country of origin.

Design and illustration: Peter Gates www.petergates.co.uk

Printed and bound in China by C & C Offset Printing Co., Ltd.

The author would like to thank Saskia Gwinn and Ruth Dix for their editorial energies and expertise, and Peter Gates for fitting everything so beautifully on the page. Thanks also to his parents for early inspirations, and to Kathy for wise words throughout.

This book is for Florence.

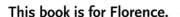

Introduction

Have you ever watched a nature programme on TV and wondered why all the best wildlife seems to be in other parts of the world?

Well, good news: it isn't! Look closer and you'll find nature is pretty impressive here too. Did you know, for example, that a bumblebee beats its wings over 200 times per second as it buzzes from flower to flower? Or that basking sharks longer than minibuses cruise around our coast every summer?

Surprised? Don't be. Just get outside and see it all for yourself. This book is packed with ideas for getting stuck into nature all year round. And you don't need to live in the countryside or visit a special nature reserve. Turn the pages to find out just how much amazing stuff is happening right on your doorstep.

You will also learn some fun ways to give nature a helping hand, such as feeding birds or building a hedgehog box, and pick up some special skills, like attracting moths at night or camouflaging yourself in the forest.

And don't worry if the weather keeps you stuck indoors. There's something in this book for every occasion. Keep it with you: you never know when you might need it.

Mike Unwin has been fascinated by nature ever since he first grew front legs and hopped out of the pond. His books for children include *The RSPB Children's Guide to Birdwatching*, *Endangered Species* and *Climate Change*, and he writes regularly for *Bird Life*, the magazine of RSPB Wildlife Explorers. Mike lives in Brighton, where he keeps an eye out for dolphins from the beach.

SPRING March–May

See the first apple blossom.

Search for snowdrops.

Spot the first summer visitor.

Watch birds singing and showing off their colours.

See birds gathering nest material.

SUMMER June–August

Watch flowers attract insects to their nectar.

Find wildflowers in a meadow.

Find juicy fruits and berries.

Look out for fledglings.

Watch swifts catch insects high overhead.

AUTUMN September–November

Find juicy fruits and berries.

See how plants disperse their seeds.

Spot fungi popping up all over.

Look out for jays collecting acorns.

Listen to tawny owls calling at night.

WINTER December–February

See which trees keep their leaves.

Look for winter buds on trees.

Follow a feeding party through the woods.

Count the birds on your garden feeder.

Marvel at a starling roost.

Look out for frogspawn.

Watch toads migrate to their breeding ponds.

Look out for adders emerging from hibernation.

Spot the first brimstone butterfly.

Watch bumblebees out and about.

Scan the sea for whales and dolphins.

Look out for bats on warm evenings.

Spot badgers and foxes with their cubs.

Look out for caterpillars.

See moths visit lights and flowers after dark.

Discover rock-pool life at the seashore.

Listen to red deer at the rut.

Watch grey seals with their pups around the coast.

Find ladybirds gathering to hibernate.

Watch butterflies and wasps on rotten fruit.

See spiders spinning their webs all over.

Watch grey squirrels chase each other through the trees.

Spot a stoat in its white winter coat.

Look for hibernating butterflies in your shed.

Go beachcombing after winter storms.

Start a nature diary

You may notice that this book keeps telling you to write things down. But where should you write them? In your nature diary, of course.

What you need

A good strong notebook – preferably spiral-bound, and not too small. A sketchbook has thick paper, which is good for drawing and sticking things in. You also need pens and pencils – and maybe paints, glue and sticky tape.

What to write

What you put in your wildlife diary is really up to you. You could keep a record of everything you see and find – or you could also write down your thoughts and feelings about nature. You could do it every day or just when you go on holiday.

Don't forget!

Your records should always include:

- Date
- Place
- Time of day
- Weather
- Habitat (the sort of environment: woods, meadow, pond and so on)

Make it fun

Make your diary look fantastic! Try some of these ideas:

Pictures
Use your diary to draw or paint things that you've seen. Or cut out pictures that you have made elsewhere and stick them in.

Photos
Cut out photos from magazines. Or, better still, print out your own snaps and stick them in.

Bits and bobs
Stick in interesting natural objects that you find, such as leaves or feathers – as long as they're flat enough!

Cool cover
Why not give your diary a personal touch by decorating the cover? An extra clear plastic cover will also protect it on nature trips.

TOP TIP

Why not use your camera phone to snap nature pics? You can download your best ones, print them out and stick them in.

Getting started

Here's a sample diary page to give you some ideas.

Garden Shed

Ivy grows here

Date: 25 September

Time: 3.00pm

Place: My back garden – the ivy behind the shed

Weather: Sunny and dry

Brick wall

A big, colourful butterfly was feeding on the ivy berries.

Only saw its underside so don't know what kind it was.

Took this photo so I can look it up later.

Also a woodpigeon flew away. It made a big clap with its

wings. I think this feather comes from its tail.

Must get a book that shows the underside of butterflies.

Spring

Spring is in the air. Longer days and warmer weather are stirring new life in the soil. Birds are singing, bees are buzzing, buds are bursting, and blossom is blooming. Soon winter will be just a dark, chilly memory.

For nature this is the busiest season of the year: everything is preparing to reproduce – by making flowers, laying eggs or having babies. So why not get outside and catch the action? There are woods to explore, seeds to plant and frogspawn to find.

Or if those April showers keep you stuck indoors, then you could keep busy with a spring project. Draw a wildlife map of your area, make a weather vane or build a special home for watching worms.

Just turn the page for lots of fun ways to make the most of spring.

Signs of spring

Some say spring starts on 1st March. Others say the 21st. But nature gets going as soon as warmer weather and longer days mean winter is almost over.

Spring spotter

You can decide for yourself when spring has started by looking out for some of these clues.

Frogspawn

Early bloomers

Some flowers, such as snowdrops and crocuses, burst out extra early. Trees have flowers too: hazels may hang their catkins from February, and April brings the first apple blossom.

Busy buzzers

Once the flowers are out you can bet the insects will follow. Look out for bumblebees, and early butterflies such as brimstones.

Hop it

Frogs and toads usually begin breeding in February. They make their way to ponds, where each female lays thousands of eggs in a bubbly jelly called spawn. Frogspawn comes in clumps, toad spawn in strings.

Dropping in

Migrating birds fly all the way from Africa to get here for spring. Some, such as this swallow, may arrive in late March. Others, such as swifts, wait until May. If you're near the coast, look out for terns – they're like lightweight seagulls, with black caps and pointy tails.

DID YOU KNOW? There are 22 species of bumblebee in Britain.

TOP TIP

You can identify a tree by the shape of its leaves. Check out the tree spotter's guide on page 17.

LOG IT Signs of spring

Why not find out exactly how early spring is starting? Note down the first date on which you see each sign. You could take a picture and add it to your nature diary. Remember: the further north you live, the later spring starts.

Flower e.g. daffodil, snowdrop

Date first seen

Blossom e.g. apple, blackthorn

Date first seen (date/month/year)

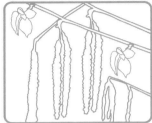

Catkin e.g. hazel, willow

Date first seen (date/month/year)

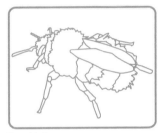

Bumblebee

Date first seen (date/month/year)

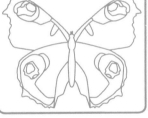

Butterfly e.g. peacock, brimstone

Date first seen (date/month/year)

Migrant bird e.g. swallow, tern

Date first seen (date/month/year)

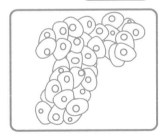

Frogspawn or toad spawn

Date first seen (date/month/year)

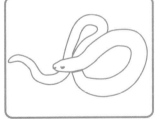

Reptile e.g. slow worm

Date first seen (date/month/year)

Anything else?

Date first seen (date/month/year)

Send it in

Your information could be important to scientists. When you've completed the chart above (or on 1 May, whichever comes first), you could send in your dates to **www.bbc.co.uk/springwatch**. Don't forget to give your address.

Dawn chorus

Birds are seriously noisy in spring. Just listen to them warbling away around your school and garden. And out in the countryside they're even noisier.

Walk in the woods

You can hear a real performance if you take a walk in the woods one fine April morning. First the bad news: you'll need to get up early. Very early. Birds sing best around dawn, when less noise and disturbance means they can hear each other more easily. The good news? You can hear them better then, too.

You will need

Warm clothes (dawn can be chilly)

A packed breakfast (make it the night before)

Binoculars (helpful, but not essential)

Ears

Song thrush

What to do

Walk slowly and quietly along a woodland path. You will hear birds everywhere: some close, some far away. Find a good, comfortable place to sit and listen.

At first all those different songs are a bit confusing. Concentrate on just one to start with. With luck you will soon spot the singer (this is where binoculars come in handy). If not, then walk slowly towards the sound – stopping if the singing stops – until you get a better view. When you know what it is, you can move on to the next sound.

Some birds, such as great tits, sing one simple phrase over and over. Others, such as robins, make up their songs as they go along – though they always follow a similar pattern.

TOP TIP

Try cupping your folded hands behind your ears and pointing yourself straight at the sound. This makes it seem louder and helps cut out other noise.

Remember the song

Identifying the singer helps fix the song in your head. Here are some tips for remembering who's who.

1 Think of something the song sounds like. A great tit's simple two-note song sounds a bit like "Teacher, teacher".

2 Remember how the song *feels*: a robin's song may feel a bit sad; a wren's is more frantic.

3 Concentrate on learning just one song at a time.

4 Start with birds around your garden or school – the ones you hear most. Once you are familiar with these, anything new or different will stand out.

WHY DO BIRDS SING? FOCUS

Usually it is just males that sing – like this wren. They do it to claim a patch of ground and keep away rivals, so the song really means "Keep out, this is mine!" The singer also aims to attract a female, so that the pair can get together and raise young. This is why birdsong is loudest in early spring – at the start of the breeding season.

LOG IT Bird talk

USE YOUR NATURE DIARY

Listen to the songs or calls of these common birds and think of something they might be saying. Make a note on this chart.

Bird	What it sounds like
Great tit	Teacher teacher
Collared dove	
Chaffinch	
Wren	
Blackbird	

Budding enthusiasts

While you were out listening to birds, did you notice the trees? You don't even have to visit the woods: leaves are bursting out on every street. Take a look.

A new leaf

Leaves come from buds. Buds are those little knobs that stick out along twigs and branches. They can be green, red, hairy or sticky, depending on the type of tree. Inside, protected by their tough, scaly jackets, the new leaves have been furled up all winter just waiting for spring. Now they are raring to go.

Buds at the tip of a branch are called terminal buds. They show where the tree stopped growing last season and where it is ready to start again. Buds on the side of the branch are called lateral buds; the larger ones usually contain flowers while the smaller ones contain leaves.

Bursting out

Buds start opening as soon as the days start getting longer. Look closely and you will see the tips of the scales coming apart and new leaves or blossoms emerging.

Try collecting a few growing twigs with buds on from different trees around you. Put each one in a glass or jar of water and watch what happens. Note down in your nature diary everything you see.

Apple blossom

A peek inside

Pick a good fat bud from a tree (a horse chestnut bud is perfect). Then use a sharp knife to cut it carefully in half lengthwise. Look inside: you should be able to see the tiny furled-up leaves. Use a magnifying glass for an even closer look.

Tree spotter's guide

The easiest way to tell trees apart is by the shape of their leaves. Here are some common ones to get you started:

Oak

Horse chestnut

Sycamore

Beech

Ash

Hazel

Hawthorn

Silver birch

LOG IT Leaf log

Keep an eye on trees near where you live and write down in your nature diary the first date on which you see new leaves or flowers.

USE YOUR NATURE DIARY

Tree	Date of first leaf	Date of first flower
Oak		
Apple		
Horse chestnut		
Sycamore		
Cherry		
Beech		
Ash		
Willow		
Silver birch		
Hazel		
Hawthorn		

Grow your own

Spring sunshine gets plants growing. So now is a good time to plant seeds. But would you prefer to grow something pretty or something tasty?

Super seeds

Nasturtium is a plant that you can both eat and admire: it has beautiful flowers and makes a delicious salad. And you don't have to be an expert gardener. All you need are the seeds. Just add soil, sunshine and water.

❶ Buy your nasturtium seeds from a garden centre. One packet is plenty.

❷ Wait for a warm, sunny period in early spring, when the last frost has passed. Sow your seeds in the soil: almost anywhere will do – a vegetable patch, a flowerbed, or a large pot, as long as it's sunny. Space them 20–30 cm (8–12 in) apart – or a little closer in containers. Use your finger to push each one down about 1 cm (0.5 in) into the soil.

❸ Water them at least once a week, especially if they are in containers. They love full sun, but they don't do well when it gets too dry.

❹ Don't use fertiliser. If the soil is too rich you will get more leaves than flowers.

What happens?

Nasturtium seeds germinate (put out shoots and roots) after a couple of weeks, and you should have beautiful flowers in six to eight weeks. They may spill over walls, spread across the ground or even climb up trellises, depending upon what kind you have planted.

Nursing nasturtiums

✿ Pick off the blooms once they die. This is called deadheading; it helps the plant produce more flowers.

✿ Keep them free from chemicals – and make sure nothing growing nearby is sprayed with chemicals.

✿ If you don't have a garden, you can grow your nasturtiums in a pot indoors – or make a lovely window box.

 **Plants in progress**

Keep a note of how your nasturtiums get along.

Date seeds planted

Date first shoots appear

Date first leaves appear

Date first flowers appear

Colour of flowers

Date last flowers died

Date of your first nasturtium salad

Recipe

Nasturtium mayonnaise

Nasturtium leaves and flowers have a nice peppery flavour, especially the fresh ones. You could add them to a green leaf salad or chop them up into pasta salads. You could even use them to make your own mayonnaise.

Ingredients

1 cup	mayonnaise
¼ tsp.	finely chopped garlic
2 tsp.	coarsely chopped capers
⅓ tsp.	grated lemon peel
2 tsp.	chopped nasturtium leaves

Mix all the ingredients together. Keep in the fridge until ready to use. Use on seafood or on any sandwiches, just like any mayonnaise. Perfect for picnics.

DID YOU KNOW? Explorers discovered nasturtiums in the jungles of Peru and Mexico in the 16th century.

Look local

How can you make regular wildlife diary entries? By making regular wildlife trips – of course! No need to travel far. Wherever you live there is wildlife nearby.

Patch work

Find a local place that you like and keep going back. Wildlife watchers call this a 'local patch'. A park, golf course or meadow will do – anywhere with a little greenery. It should be small enough to get to know but big enough to support lots of wildlife. Try to find somewhere that:

- has some different habitats, such as a bit of woodland and a bit of scrub
- has some open water, such as a pond or stream
- is just a short walk, cycle or bus ride away
- needs no more than one hour for a visit.

Watching a local patch means you get to know its wildlife really well. The important thing is to keep visiting: go at different times of day and different times of year. That way you will see as much as possible, and you will notice how things change through the seasons.

Safety first

Ask a grown-up to help choose your local patch and ALWAYS tell them when you are going there. Better still, take a grown-up with you.

What to look for

Anything and everything: birds, mammals, insects, flowers, fungi, seeds, tracks and signs – you name it. Note it all down in your nature diary. Try to find out:

What plants grow there?
For example, a group of birch trees or a hawthorn hedge.

Where does the wildlife live?
For example, the moorhen by the pond, the grey squirrels in the beech trees.

When do you see the wildlife?
For example, frogs in spring, bats in summer.

Pipistrelle bat

Make a wildlife map

You could make a wildlife map of your local patch to record exactly where you saw things – and show other people, too. Use a big, strong piece of paper (at least A2 size). Then fix it to the wall and use blu-tack or tape to stick up your own notes and pictures. Better still, fix your map onto a corkboard and pin them up.

Your map should show main features, such as any trees, water, hedges, paths, roads or buildings. Here's how it might look.

Interesting fungus

19 May
Saw bright spotty moths – looked like this:

rough grass

Tall bracken

Birch wood

Bull rushes

Path to hill

Badgers set

Clay bank

Pond

To road

Footpath

Holly

Water meadow

3 May
Fluffy black feathers all over the ground here. Think the sparrowhawk caught a blackbird.

TOP TIP

Sketch the map outline first to get the rough size and shape, then fill in the details. You could look at a real map to help make sure that everything is roughly the right distance apart.

Tadpole surprise!

Remember those first signs of spring? One was probably frogspawn. This strange jelly appears in ponds from February. So what happens to it?

Eggs to legs

Frogspawn, is frogs' eggs. One day some of those tiny black dots will become full-grown frogs. You can watch for yourself how this happens.

You will need

A jam jar
A lid that you can make holes in
A large see-through container, at least 15cm (6 in) deep

❶ Use a jam jar to scoop up half a cup of frogspawn from a pond. Scoop up some pondweed, too, and keep it all in the pond water.

❷ Put it into a container at home with a wide top (so plenty of oxygen can get into the water). Put in one or two stones that stick out above the surface of the water: the froglets will need them later.

❸ Watch the tadpoles as they hatch from the frogspawn. At first they eat the jelly, then they eat tiny pond animals. Keep them supplied with fresh pondweed and pond water.

❹ As their back legs appear, feed them with little pieces of raw meat. But don't leave uneaten bits to rot in the water. Fish flakes are also good food.

❺ Once their front legs begin to grow and their tails start to shrink, the tadpoles will climb up onto the rocks. Cover the top of the container so they don't escape (but make holes in the lid to allow them to breathe).

Once their tails disappear it's time to release your froglets carefully back into the wild. **ALWAYS RETURN THEM TO THE POND WHERE YOU FOUND THEM**. They will soon hop off to start the tricky job of growing up into frogs.

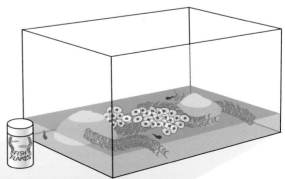

Young frog

BREATHING CHANGES

FOCUS

DID YOU KNOW? Only about one egg in 400 will survive to become an adult frog. **DID YOU KNOW?**

Frog-wise

➤ Frogspawn comes in clumps; toad spawn comes in strings.

➤ NEVER use tap water. It has chemicals that might harm the tadpoles.

➤ Do not handle froglets. They are very delicate and you may damage them.

Young tadpoles breathe underwater through gills (those feathery things behind the head), like fishes do. At nine weeks they lose their gills and develop lungs, so they must swim to the surface to breathe air. Adult frogs continue to breathe through their lungs and can also receive oxygen through their moist skin.

LOG IT Tadpole growth chart

USE YOUR NATURE DIARY

Use this chart to record what you see. Carry on in your nature diary if you need more space.

Date frogspawn first seen:
(date / month / year)

Location of frogspawn:
(   )

Date tadpoles first emerge:
(date / month / year)

Date tadpoles first seen breathing air:
(date / month / year)

Date tadpoles first show back legs:
(date / month / year)

Date tadpoles first show front legs:
(date / month / year)

Date tadpoles first lose their tail:
(date / month / year)

Date froglets first leave the water:
(date / month / year)

Date you return froglets to their pond:
(date / month / year)

Total number of days, from frogspawn to froglet:
(   )

frogspawn

tadpoles

breathing

back legs

front legs

lose their tail

Draw a frog

Frogs look great, with their huge webbed feet and big bulgy eyes. But they're not so easy to draw. Here's one way to do it.

Step by step

You will need paper and a pencil – of course! And coloured pencils, if you want to colour it in. Then just follow these five simple steps.

Step 1 ▶

Draw two egg-shaped circles: one for the body, and a smaller one for the head positioned above it and to the right. Allow plenty of space: this frog is going to be big!

Step 2 ▶

Draw a line that links the top of the two eggs together. This is the top of the frog's back and head. Don't miss the little peak along the back and the bulge where the eye sticks up. Continue the line around the snout to make the throat. Go over this line gently until you think it looks right.

Step 3 ▶

Now add the legs. The front leg joins just below the throat. Look carefully to see how the back right leg (the one you can see) is folded. The other back leg is mostly hidden by the body.

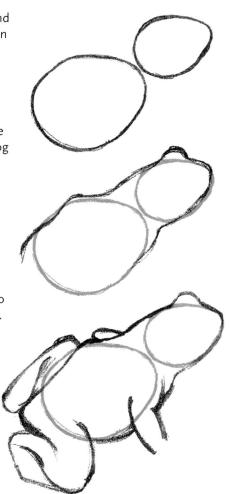

Step 4 ▼

Add the eyes, mouth and feet. The mouth is a straight line that reaches almost to the top of the front leg. The eye has a line above it to show the bulgy socket. Each foot has three toes showing. On the back foot the middle toe is longest. The front foot is turned in slightly.

Step 5 ▼

The finishing touches. Add a pupil to the eye and webbing to the back feet (but NOT the front feet). Now, if you like, you can colour it and add some markings. Give it a greenish body, with a yellow tummy and a white throat. Add darker stripes on the legs, spots on the body and a patch around the eye.

Get sketching

The best way to draw a frog is to use a real live one as your model. Try taking a sketchbook, rubber and pencils to a place where you sometimes see frogs.

Sit quietly and wait until one appears, then draw what you see. You may not be able to see all of it – it may hop away or plop underwater before you finish. No problem: you don't *have* to finish. Just start another one when it appears again.

Don't bother rubbing anything out, either. Just keep drawing, as quickly as you can. Soon you will get the hang of it.

AMPHIBIANS

Frogs, along with toads and newts, are amphibians. Amphibians live partly on land and partly on water, and lay their eggs in water. They have soft, moist skin.

Nest building

Spring sees birds rushing to build their nests. There is no time to waste: chicks must hatch in time for summer, when food is most plentiful.

Hidden away

By early April most birds will be hard at work building. Many hide their nests away in secret places, such as deep in a thorny hedge or high in the fork of a tree. If you find one, STAY AWAY! Otherwise they might abandon their work.

You shouldn't look for nests, but you can still keep an eye out for signs of nest building. Birds often give you a clue with the way they behave:

○ **Carrying twigs**
  Many birds, from blackbirds to herons, carry sticks and twigs to build their nests.

○ **Visiting holes**
  Many birds, including blue tits and starlings, nest in tree holes. Some, such as kingfishers, use holes in sandbanks.

○ **Perching beside puddles**
  Swallows and house martins fly down to puddles to collect mud, which they use to build their nests under the walls of buildings.

○ **Carrying seaweed**
  Gulls, cormorants and other seabirds collect seaweed from the seashore to build their nests.

Rook-watch

Rooks are not so secretive about their nest building. Many pairs nest together in noisy colonies, called rookeries. They usually choose tall trees on farmland and build their nests high in the branches. Building starts when the branches are bare, so you can watch the nests get bigger as the birds keep bringing twigs.

Grey heron

Material benefits

You can help birds out by supplying extra building materials. Put it where cats can't reach and it won't blow away, such as stuffed into tree crevices or hung in small baskets. The following things might come in useful:

- String
- Bits of wool
- Horse hair (or your own hair, if you've had it cut)
- Fur (combed from your dog or cat)
- Feathers (from an old pillow or duvet)
- Shredded paper

 **LOG IT** Nesting notes

Use your nature diary to keep notes of nesting behaviour. Here are some things you could record:

Date	Type of bird	Behaviour	Where
9 April	Starling	Carrying twigs	Roof of school

FEATHER BED  **FOCUS**

Long-tailed tits build a complicated nest deep in a thick bush. They start with a foundation of moss. Then they add sticky cobwebs to bind it together. Next they cover the outside with lichen, for camouflage. Finally they add a soft lining of feathers — more than 1,000 — to keep the eggs and chicks warm.

Make a weather vane

April showers again, and you're stuck indoors. Wouldn't life be easier with your own weather forecast? Well you can start by making a weather vane.

Pointing at the wind

A weather vane measures wind direction. The wind makes it spin around and point in the direction the wind is coming from. This tells you what the wind might be like. For example, a south wind is usually warm (because it comes from the south), while a north wind is usually cold (because ... you guessed it!)

All weather vanes have an arrow-shaped end, which turns into the wind, and a wider end, which catches the breeze and makes it turn.

You will need

Cardboard
(an old cardboard box will do)

Pen

Scissors

Tape

Thin stick (a wooden skewer/ kebab stick is perfect)

Drinking straw

Hammer and nail

Plastic soft drink bottle with cap

Sand

Compass

Here's how you can make your own, using just cardboard.

❶ Mark out a large arrow on the cardboard to the shape and measurements shown below. Then cut it out.

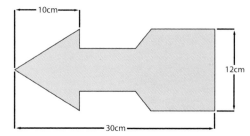

❷ Tape one end of the wooden skewer to the arrow and insert the other end in the straw. The skewer should turn freely inside the straw.

❸ Make a hole in the bottle cap (a grown-up will help), just large enough to hold the straw firmly. Then push the straw through. Fill the bottom of the bottle with sand.

❹ Fit the straw into the bottle and do up the cap. The straw should be upright, the arrow should turn freely and the bottle should remain steady.

5 Use a compass or a map to work out where north is (maps always have north at the top of the page). Then mark the directions of north, south, east and west on the bottle – or on the surface where you place it.

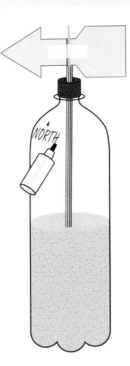

Set it up

Place your weather vane somewhere it will catch the breeze – on top of a wall is good – and watch what happens. Remember, the arrow always points in the direction that the wind is coming from. Bring it in when it rains.

Customise!

Weather vanes work in many different shapes and materials. You could make one out of wood, if you're good at woodwork, or decorate it with a cockerel – like the ones you see on church roofs. The important things are that the arrow turns freely, you know where north is, and that it doesn't blow away.

LOG IT Weather report

Try checking you weather vane twice a day, and keep this up for a week. Note down the wind direction and any other weather you notice, too – such as whether it is sunny or raining.

Day	Time	Wind	Weather
Monday			
Tuesday			
Wednesday			
Thursday			
Friday			

Worm wonders

What are the most important animals in any garden? Robins, you might think, or hedgehogs. Wrong! The answer is wriggly, slimy and right under your feet.

Wriggly revelations

Worms are amazing. Here are some facts I bet you didn't know:

- It takes worms about five years to create 2.5 cm (1 in) of good topsoil. Without worms it would take over 500 years.

- The number of worms in the soil depends on its quality, but an average garden lawn probably has about 25 worms in every 30 cubic centimeters (2 in³).

- Earthworms move using four tiny bristles on each segment of their body. These bristles help to anchor them in the soil if a bird tries to pull them out.

- A worm is both male and female. This means each worm can mate with any other one.

- Every single bit of soil in a park or garden has been through a worm at least once.

- Earthworms have no eyes or ears, so they cannot see or hear. They mostly find their way around by touch.

- The largest earthworm ever found was in South Africa. It measured a whopping 6.7 metres (22 feet) from nose to tail.

Mixing it

Earthworms make the soil healthier by processing dead plant and animal matter through their bodies. They also mix the soil up and drain it. Healthy soil means more plants grow, and more plants mean more animals. So everything really depends upon worms.

PADDLING **FOCUS**

Have you ever noticed gulls paddling their feet up and down on a wet field? This helps them to catch worms: the vibrations made by their webbed feet help attract the worms to the surface. You can watch plovers and other wading birds doing the same thing on wet sand and mud.

Make your own wormery

First ... catch your worms

They say the early bird catches the worm. Here are three ways you can find some for yourself.

- **Habitat hunt** Turn over stones, look under leaf litter and dig in bare earth.
- **Soaking** Water forces worms to the surface. So hunt for them on a rainy night – or pour a bucket of water onto a patch of soil and see if it brings them up.
- **Under the carpet** Leave a piece of old carpet on the soil for a day or so, then lift it up and collect any worms that have appeared underneath.

What to do

You will need:

Two-litre plastic bottle
Large plant pot filled with soil
Black paper, cardboard or material
Soft sand
Crushed chalk (blackboard chalk will do)
Dead leaves
Ten earthworms (alive!)
A marker pen

❶ Cut the top and bottom off the plastic bottle to make a tall cylinder.

❷ Put the earthworms into the plant pot.

❸ Place the cylinder on top of the soil and fill it with alternate layers of soil, crushed chalk and soft sand. Each layer should be about 3 cm (1 in) deep.

❹ Mark the levels of each layer on the outside of the cylinder with the marker.

❺ Break the dead leaves into smallish pieces and scatter them on top.

❻ Keep the light out of the cylinder by wrapping the black paper or material around it and placing the black card over the top.

❼ Keep everything damp – not wet – and leave for several days in a cool place.

Result!

Remove the covering from your cylinder after about a week. What do you notice? With luck, the worms will have tunnelled through the earth, churning up your neat layers and dragging down leaves from the surface. Record your observations in your nature diary.

Now release your earthworms back into the garden where they can continue their good work – but not when any hungry birds are watching.

Riverside ramble

Spring is a great time to walk along a riverbank. Find a river near you; a small stream or even a canal will do. Then see what wildlife you can find.

Mallard with ducklings

Water vole

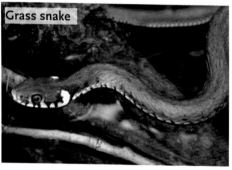

Grass snake

Water wildlife

Many animals live on or beside rivers. Here are some to look out for:

Birds

Most birds will be busy breeding. The **mallard** is the UK's most common duck. Its young may hatch as early as March. Look out for fluffy chicks following their mum. The **moorhen** has long toes for clambering around in the riverside vegetation. Look out for its sticky-up white tail. A speeding flash of brilliant blue might be a **kingfisher** in a hurry. This shy bird is more common than you might think. Look out along canals – even in towns.

Water vole Look out for a small, furry nose swimming across the water: it might be a water vole. This rare rodent likes quiet waterways, where it makes its home in riverbank tunnels. Don't mistake it for a brown rat, which can also swim. Small, hidden ears and a shortish tail means vole; big ears and a long pink tail means rat.

Grass snake See those gleaming coils slithering through the wet grass? It's a grass snake. You can tell it by its yellow collar. Grass snakes are perfectly harmless to people – although not to frogs, which they catch and swallow whole.

Dragon or damsel?

Bzzzzz! What was that –
a big insect or a tiny plane?
It must be a dragonfly –
or maybe a damselfly. But
how to tell which is which?
Easy! Dragonflies perch
with their wings sticking
out sideways, and fly fast
and straight; damselflies
fold their wings together
over their back, and have a
weaker, more fluttery flight.

Dragonfly

Damselfly

Whistle while you walk

Grass grows long on a riverside path, so why not try this
noisy trick? Pick a flat, smooth blade of grass and break
off a piece from the middle, about 5 cm (2 in) long. Lace
your fingers together, thumbs sticking up, and insert the
grass sideways into the small gap between your thumbs –
leaving a tiny crack on either side (for the air to get past).
Then blow on the grass.

Keep trying, adjusting the grass, until you get a piercing
whistle – a bit like an out-of-tune saxophone. This is just
how a saxophone works, using a thin reed in
the mouthpiece.

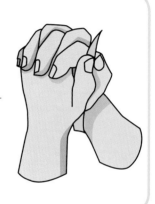

LOG IT Riverside spotter

Make a note of your riverside sightings. If you need
more space continue in your nature diary. Which list is longest?

DIARY USE YOUR NATURE

Birds	
Insects	
Plants	

Web of life

How do you think all those riverbank animals get along together? The answer is by eating each other! Here's how it works.

Fitting together

In nature every animal must feed on another animal or plant in order to survive. In turn it may become a meal for something else. All these plants and animals make up a community called an ecosystem. Every different environment, from a river to a forest, has its own ecosystem, made up of the plants and animals that live there. An ecosystem is like a jigsaw, in which every living thing is a piece.

Web of life

A diagram called a food web shows just how all the living things in any place depend upon one another for food. The food web in the picture below shows some of the plants and animals that live in or beside a river. Follow the arrows and you can see exactly who eats what.

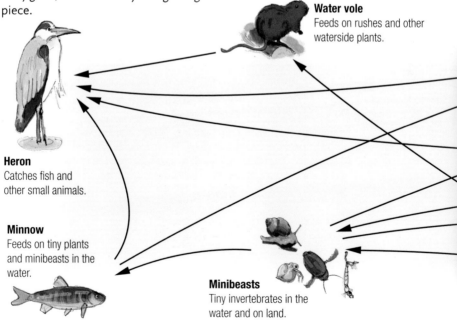

Water vole
Feeds on rushes and other waterside plants.

Heron
Catches fish and other small animals.

Minnow
Feeds on tiny plants and minibeasts in the water.

Minibeasts
Tiny invertebrates in the water and on land.

GREEN PLANTS

All food webs contain green plants. Plants are called producers: they produce food using energy from the sun. Animals are called consumers: they consume food by eating plants or other animals that have eaten plants. Without plants there would be no life on earth. Think about this next time you see somebody pulling up a thistle or chopping down a tree!

TOP TIP

The arrows on a food web always point from the food towards the thing that eats it.

Make a food web

Why not try to make a food web of your own? Write down in your nature diary all the different animals and plants that live around your home or school. Then use a big piece of paper to see how many you can connect in a food web. Each time you add a new animal, try to find it a place on your web. Here are some to start you off:

Aphid (greenfly)	Ladybird
Bird seed	Cat
Rose bush	Blackbird
Earthworm	Snail

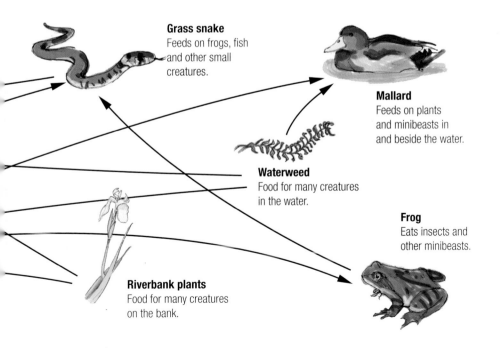

Grass snake
Feeds on frogs, fish and other small creatures.

Mallard
Feeds on plants and minibeasts in and beside the water.

Waterweed
Food for many creatures in the water.

Frog
Eats insects and other minibeasts.

Riverbank plants
Food for many creatures on the bank.

Summer

Summer is a time of plenty: the grass is growing long, the countryside is cloaked in leaves and the mini-beasts are out in force, munching their way through all that greenery. Bigger animals, meanwhile, are busy looking after their new babies.

Now is the best time of year to look for butterflies and moths, and to find out what lurks at the bottom of a pond. And you could use those long, warm evenings to see what wildlife gets up to after dark.

Summer also means holidays – and perhaps a chance to see new wildlife at the seaside or even on a boat trip. And if you're stuck indoors, then you could make a special device for catching mini-beasts or design a wonderful wind-chime for your garden.

Just turn the page for lots of fun ways to make the most of summer.

Beachcomber

Summer at the seaside means splashing in the surf and sand between your toes. But beaches are great for nature, too. You'll be amazed at what you find.

Top to bottom

Walk along slowly scanning the ground carefully. This is called beachcombing. Look down near the water's edge, where the sand is firm and wet, and higher up, among the tangled old seaweed left behind by the tide.

Bladderwrack

This seaweed is called bladderwrack. The bubbles are full of gas that helps it to float on the surface. Try popping them. (Dry ones are easiest.)

Lugworm cast

Lugworms live in burrows under your feet. They swallow sand to extract food then squirt out the leftover into little coils on the surface.

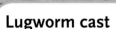

Seashell

Every seashell once contained a living, soft-bodied animal. This is a razor shell. A tiny jet of water squirting up from the sand shows where one is burrowing down.

Sea urchin case

This lumpy, empty egg-like case was once covered in spines. It breaks easily, so you might just find bits and pieces. Sea urchins graze on seaweed in rock pools.

Crab shell

This shell belonged to a common shore crab. As crabs grow bigger they shed their shells regularly and grow new, bigger ones. A new shell takes several days to harden. Look out in rock pools for living crabs.

Whelk egg case

This crispy, bubbly stuff is a clump of old whelk egg cases. It is empty now; the babies hatched out in the sea. Look out on the beach for the big, whitish shells of adult whelks.

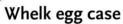

Mermaid's purse

This shiny black pouch is the empty egg case of a skate, a kind of flat fish. It is sometimes called a mermaid's purse. The arms at each corner show where it fastened to the seaweed.

Safety first

All kinds of nasty rubbish washes up on beaches, including waste from ships and towns. So never pick up anything you don't recognise. And always wash your hands after beachcombing.

Seashell wind-chime

Seashells can make a musical wind-chime for your house or classroom. Hang it up outside and every time a breeze blows you'll hear the sound of the sea.

How to make it

This is the perfect way to make use of all those shells you brought back from the beach.

You will need

Ten or more seashells

Coloured wool

Plastic coffee jar lid

White glue

Hole punch

Paint

Other decorative beach items

❶ Clean the shells well in hot soapy water and let them dry completely.

❷ Cut ten pieces of wool in different lengths, from 10 cm to 30 cm (4 in to 12 in), with which to attach the shells. Cut another piece about 30 cm (12 in) long from which to hang the finished wind-chime.

❸ Punch two holes at opposite edges of the lid. (Ask an adult for help with this part.) This is for hanging the wind-chime.

❹ Punch ten evenly spaced holes around the outer edge of the lid. This will be where you attach the shells.

❺ Glue one end of a piece of wool to the inside of each seashell. Leave it to dry.

❻ Decorate the lid. You could use paint, or stick other items on, such as crab shells and feathers. Leave it to dry.

TOP TIP

Use only your best shells. Flattish ones, such as scallops or oysters, work really well. Try to find ones that are not chipped or broken.

7 Push the loose end of each piece of wool through one of the holes around the base, then secure with a knot.

8 Once the shells are attached, thread the final long piece of wool through the two holes for hanging the chime. Tie the wool securely using large knots.

9 Now you can hang up your wind-chime. Try your bedroom ceiling, or maybe a tree outside.

SHELLS FOCUS

Seashells were once the home of small, soft-bodied, snail-like animals. The ones that open up into two hinged halves, such as cockles, are called bivalves. The ones that consist of just a single coiled shell, such as limpets, are called univalves.

LOG IT

Which shell?

Here are five common types of shell. Do they help you identify the ones you have collected? Make a note of where and when you found each.

Cockle — Where? When?

Mussel — Where? When?

Limpet — Where? When?

Whelk — Where? When?

Scallop — Where? When?

Continue this activity in your nature diary. You could take a photo of different shells you find, or sketch a picture.

Growing wild

Trim, snip, buzz! Gardeners like to keep things spick and span. But animals prefer messier gardens, where they can find good hideaways and lots of food.

Leave it!

Help animals by making your own wild patch. Just choose a hidden spot where wild plants can grow undisturbed and leave it to grow naturally. Your parents or teacher can keep everywhere else as neat as they like, just so long as they leave your patch alone.

Goldfinch on a teasel

Let it grow

New plants will soon start to appear in your wild patch. These may be 'weeds' to gardeners, but to wildlife they mean food and shelter. Here are some to look out for:

Dandelions are usually among the first newcomers. Look out for their long leaves with toothy edges, and their tall yellow flowers.

Thistles and teasels may just be annoying prickles to us, but the leaves are a salad for slugs and snails, and the seeds provide an autumn feast for finches. Thistle flowers offer nectar to insects.

Nettles may eventually begin to appear in damp, shady corners, such as behind a shed. Look out for the bristly black caterpillars of butterflies, such as the small tortoiseshell and peacock, that feed on the leaves. Nettle beds also make a great hiding place for hedgehogs. Just be careful of those stinging leaves.

TOP TIP

Try lying down and looking at your lawn from ground level. The grass stems seem enormous – like a jungle. It's a perfect home for mini-beasts.

Other garden goodies

There are many ways to help wildlife in your garden:

Plant berry bushes
Berries provide juicy treats for thrushes and other birds in winter. Berry bushes are also great places for insects when other plants are bare.

Leave deadheads
Old blooms, such as those of sunflowers and hollyhocks, are packed with tasty seeds for many small creatures.

Save ivy
This fantastic wildlife plant offers nest sites for birds, nectar for insects, and winter hibernation spots for butterflies and other mini-beasts.

Comma butterfly on ivy

Make a log pile

A pile of old logs can make a nice finishing touch to your wild patch. Fungi may grow on the logs, helping to break them down into the soil again.

The rotten wood provides food for burrowing animals inside, such as stag beetle larvae, while the damp, hidden crevices make hiding places for mini-beasts, such as woodlice and centipedes. A toad may even find a home underneath. Take a careful peek every now and then, but don't disturb them too often.

LOG IT Wild patch records

Keep a record of the wildlife discoveries you make in your wild patch. The first one is an example to get you started.

Date	Mini-Beasts	Birds	Amphibians	Plants	Other
8 June	Speckled wood butterfly		Dandelion flowers appeared		

USE YOUR NATURE DIARY

Bug hunt

Summer is the best season for spotting mini-beasts. You'll be amazed at what you find lurking in the greenery if you just rummage around.

Look closer!

Here are some mini-beasts to look out for:

Caterpillars

The larvae of butterflies, moths and sawflies. Look for looper caterpillars, which move by arching their body into a loop.

Crickets

Just like grasshoppers, but with much longer antennae (feelers). They tend to live in the grass.

Shield bug

A bit like a beetle, but with a shield-shaped body and sharp mouthparts for sucking the sap out of plants.

Ladybirds

Colourful beetles that feed mostly on aphids (greenflies). They are mostly red but can be other colours, such as yellow or black, and different species have different numbers of spots.

Crab spider

Small spiders that don't build webs but lie in wait in the leaves, ready to ambush insects.

MINI-BEASTS (FOCUS)

The scientific name for all mini-beasts is invertebrates, which means animals without a backbone. There are thousands of different types. You can sort them into basic groups by counting their legs.

Insects	6 legs
Spiders	8 legs
Woodlice	14 legs
Centipede	100 legs or more
Millipede	700 legs or more

Beating about the bush

Trees and bushes are full of mini-beasts. And a good way to find them is with a little gentle shake-up. Don't shake too hard, you don't want to harm them!

You will need

An old sheet
(a light colour is best)

A stick

Some clean, empty plastic containers
(old margarine tubs work well)

White plastic spoons

A small fine paintbrush

What to do

❶ Find a good bush or an overhanging leafy branch – it could be in your garden, a park, or the countryside. One with some flowers or blossom, such as hawthorn, is best.

❷ Lay the sheet out underneath.

❸ Give the branch a short, firm shake – or a sharp tap with your stick. You don't want to break the branch, but if you tap too gently the mini-beasts will just cling on. The idea is to take them by surprise.

❹ As the mini-beasts drop onto your sheet, use the paintbrush to flick them into your spoon and, from there, place them in the pots. For very small ones you could use a pooter (see pages 46–47).

LOG IT Weird and wonderful

Imagine if mini-beasts were the size of humans. Take a picture of the strangest one you find and stick it here. Zoom in as close as you can to make it look really weird.

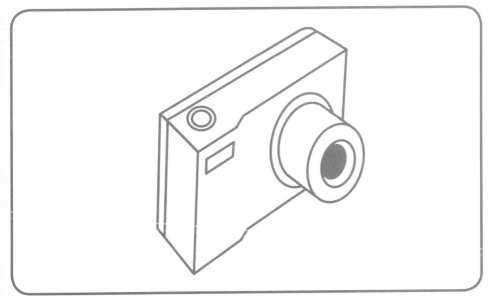

Make a pooter

Butterflies, bumblebees and other bigger mini-beasts are easy to observe. But how can you get a look at the really tiny ones? Here's something to try.

What to do

Scientists use a simple device called a pooter, which sucks up small bugs just like a miniature vacuum cleaner.

You will need

A small, clear jar

75 cm (30 in) of thin plastic tubing, about 5 mm (0.2 in) in diameter (available from DIY shops or garages)

A small scrap of muslin or j-cloth

An elastic band

A piece of card

A hole punch

Sellotape

A blob of Plasticine or Blu-tak

1 Cut the tube into two pieces: one 50 cm (20 in) long, the other 25 cm (10 in) long.

2 Use the elastic band to secure the scrap of cloth over one end of the shorter tube.

3 Cut a piece of card to fit over the top of the jar or bottle, then punch two holes in it.

4 Push the two pieces of tube through the two holes in the card and position the card over the top of the jar. The covered end of the short tube should be on the inside of the jar.

To look at your mini-beasts really close-up you need a magnifying glass. Small fold-up hand lenses are best: they pack away neatly into their protective case.

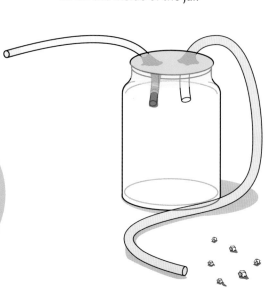

5 Using the sellotape, fasten the card to the top of the jar.

6 Fix the tubes in place using Plasticine or Blu-tak.

7 First practise using your pooter on tiny screwed-up scraps of paper. Place the long tube over one then suck on the short tube. This should pull the scrap up into the jar but the muslin will stop it entering your mouth. Success? Good. Now you are ready to catch some bugs.

Be nice to bugs

- Always release mini-beasts where you found them.
- Never leave any mini-beast in the sun for too long.
- Avoid touching mini-beasts directly: you might accidentally rub off scales or hairs, which can harm them.
- Replace any stones or logs that you turn over.

TOP TIP

If your pooter isn't working, check that the lid is fastened so that air can't get into your jar.

Pooter precautions

- Only suck up very small mini-beasts that fit the tube. Anything bigger or with long legs could get stuck or damaged.
- Don't suck too hard: you don't want to damage any of the creatures you catch.
- Try to keep the jar dry: do not blow into the tubes, as moisture will condense from your breath.
- Do not suck up wet or slimy animals, such as slugs.
- Don't keep too many mini-beasts together in the jar at once. And do not keep predators, such as spiders, together with other creatures that they might eat.

Butterfly bonanza

Summer brings butterflies fluttering about the countryside and visiting your garden. They're on the lookout for flowers – and you can help give them what they need.

Nectar delight

Butterflies like flowers because they contain nectar. Creep up quietly on one that's feeding and you'll see it uncurl its long proboscis to sip this sweet, sticky liquid. One of the very best nectar plants is buddleia: look out for feasting butterflies wherever you see its big purple flower heads.

Peacock

Bright eyespots scare away hungry birds.

Red admiral

Visits the same flowers at the same time each day.

Large white

The biggest white butterfly in your garden.

Top flowers for butterflies

Here are some good nectar plants for your school or garden. Plants that flower in spring and autumn are important, too: these help the earliest and latest butterflies of the year.

Spring flowers	Summer flowers	Autumn flowers
Oxeye daisy	Buddleia	Ivy
Pansy	Chrysanthemum	Lavender
Bugle	Cornflower	Lilac
Sweet William	Forget-me-not	Phlox
Wallflower	French Marigold	Michaelmas Daisy

Food plants

Nectar isn't all that butterflies need. They are also looking for their 'food plants' – the plants on which they lay their eggs and that provide food for their caterpillars. Each species prefers a particular plant. Large and small whites, for instance, lay their eggs under cabbage leaves, which is why they are called 'cabbage whites'. The caterpillars then munch the cabbages – making themselves very unpopular with gardeners.

Favourite food plants

Butterfly	Favourite plant
Painted lady	Thistles
Holly blue	Holly and ivy
Peacock, small tortoiseshell	Stinging nettle

GO WILD

 **FOCUS**

Now is when your wild patch comes in useful (see page 42). Wild flowers, such as dandelions, thistles, purple loosestrife, red valerian and scabious, are all butterfly favourites. Long grasses are also good food plants for many butterflies, including gatekeepers.

Boy or girl?

Male butterflies may fight over the top feeding and breeding spots. This fun trick helps you work out whether a white butterfly is male or female.

Cut out a butterfly-sized piece of white rag and attach it with an elastic band to the end of a long piece of wire. Then find a place with lots of white butterflies and wave your stick around in a jerky way. Male butterflies should soon flutter across to check out their rival – though they'll fly off once they realise their mistake. Females won't be interested at all.

TOP TIP

If you don't have flowers in your garden, try leaving out rotten fruit. Butterflies love the sugary liquids.

Pond dipping

Not all mini-beasts are hiding on your bushes and lawns. There's a whole world of them that live underwater. And the best way to find them is to go pond dipping.

What to do

Make sure you take all your gear with you. Then follow the steps below.

You will need

Permission to use the pond

A net with a handle (use a bucket and sieve if you don't have a net)

White plastic spoons

Three plastic tubs (ice-cream or margarine tubs)

Wellies and waterproofs

Sieves

Magnifying glass (or hand lens)

1 Find a pond. It could be in your garden, school or local park. A small one will do – but not a dirty one full of rubbish.

2 Approach quietly, as you may see birds, frogs or other wildlife around the edge. Wait to see if you can spot any activity on or below the surface.

Pond skater

3 Fill the tubs with clean pond water.

4 Sweep your net through the water. Empty the contents into the first tub by turning your net inside out and gently washing it in the water – or gently lift out any creatures using a plastic spoon. Some things may not look like animals at first, so give them time to move.

5 Next, try sweeping your net through the water plants, then collect what you find in a new tub of water.

6 Last, sweep up a small amount of mud from the bottom and wash this in the net before emptying the contents into a new tub.

7 Use your magnifying glass to take a good look at what you find, and record your findings in your nature diary.

8 After investigating what is in your tubs, return the water and everything inside to where you found it. Don't keep creatures out of the pond for too long.

TOP TIP

Don't just swish your net around at random. Sweeping in straight lines and a regular rhythm brings the best results.

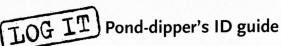 **Pond-dipper's ID guide**

Here are some creatures you might catch. Tick the box beside each one that you catch and make a note of where and when you caught it.

Water beetle
Swims using hindlegs
like flippers.
Caught? ☐ Time _____
Location _____
How many? _____

Pond skater
Skates across the surface to
catch insects that fall in.
Caught? ☐ Time _____
Location _____
How many? _____

Freshwater shrimp
Feeds near the bottom on
dead and rotten things.
Caught? ☐ Time _____
Location _____
How many? _____

Common pond snail
Common snail,
with pointed shell.
Caught? ☐ Time _____
Location _____
How many? _____

Mosquito larva
Tiny; hangs from the surface
and wriggles downwards
when disturbed.
Caught? ☐ Time _____
Location _____
How many? _____

Leech
Underwater worm that attaches
to other creatures and sucks their
blood; can stretch out long and thin.
Caught? ☐ Time _____
Location _____
How many? _____

Dragonfly nymph
Shoots out its jaws to catch other
small pond creatures; eventually
climbs out and hatches into an
adult dragonfly.
Caught? ☐ Time _____
Location _____
How many? _____

Anything else?
Make a list of anything else
you catch in your nature diary.
Sketch it or take a picture if you
don't know what it is, then
look it up later.

Safety first
Always take an adult
with you when visiting
a pond. Beware of
slippery banks and do
not enter the water.
If you have any cuts
on your hands, make
sure they are covered.
Wash your hands when
you finish.

Night watch

Go into your garden on a warm evening, just as darkness is falling. Take a torch but don't turn it on yet. Instead just sit still. What can you see and hear?

Look up

Before it gets too dark you might see or hear swifts high in the sky. These birds actually sleep in the air! They fly up to where the air is cool and circle until dawn, taking quick naps as they glide around.

Late evening also brings out insects. You might spot moths in search of nectar or swarms of tiny gnats. All these insects make a tasty meal for bats. Look carefully and you might see them flitting about in search of their prey.

Ears open

As it gets darker, forget about your eyes and just trust your ears. At first you may just hear the traffic. But there are also animals moving around. A rustle may be the sound of a cat or a fox. You might even hear the snuffle of a hedgehog.

Listen for birds, too. You may hear a blackbird or robin still singing, or – near the seaside – gulls calling from rooftops as they settle down to roost.

Echo warrior

When bats fly close by you might hear their very high-pitched squeaks. These noises bounce off surrounding objects, making little echoes that help the bat to find and catch its prey. This is called echolocation. It is so accurate that it even allows bats to catch moths in flight.

Turn on your torch

Now it's really dark and you may be feeling a bit chilly. But before you go back inside, try switching on your torch for a quick search. You may spot snails and slugs leaving their glistening trails.

Check out the pond, if you have one. Frogs may plop into the water as you approach. Many animals, such as pond snails, stay active after dark, and you might even spot a newt peering up at you.

EYE-SHINE

Your torch beam may reflect the shining eyes of a cat or fox. This 'eye-shine' is caused by light bouncing off a sort of mirror behind their eyes, called a tapetum, which helps them see after dark. Even spiders' eyes have it: look out for their faint glow among the bushes.

LOG IT Night watch

Note down everything you detect on your night watch. Use your nature diary if you need more space.

Date and time	Seen	Heard
20 July 9.45-10.15pm	New moon swifts big moth (hawk moth)	Seagulls on roof, dog barking

Make a moth lure

Night-time is moth time. Many species come out only after dark. Just like butterflies, they are looking for nectar. You can give them a helping hand.

Nectar substitute

Here's how to make your own special nectar to lure moths to your garden.

You will need

Sugar
Syrup
Fruit juice / cola
Large pan
Jam jar
Paintbrush

❶ Mix the syrup, sugar and cola or fruit juice and heat gently in the pan. An adult can help. Watch to make sure the mixture does not stick to the bottom – add water if you need to make it runnier. It has to be runny enough to use as paint.

❷ Pour the mixture into the jam jar.

❸ Just before dusk, use a paintbrush to spread the mixture onto tree trunks or fence posts at eye level.

❹ Wait for an hour then come back with a torch to see whether any moths have arrived. Check two or three times during the first two hours of darkness.

BUTTERFLY OR MOTH?

Some moths fly by day, so butterflies and moths are not always easy to tell apart. Look at the antennae (feelers): all butterflies have a little lump on the tips of theirs, while most moths don't have that lump. Male moths have feathery antennae.

FOCUS

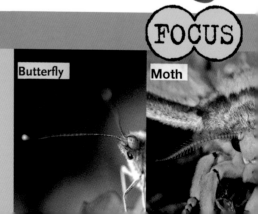

Butterfly

Moth

LOG IT Moth count

Even a small garden can have over 100 different species of moth that visit regularly, both by night and day. This chart shows six of the larger and more easily identifiable ones. Make a note of which you see, including the time, place and date.

Moth	Poplar hawk moth
Details	Large, attracted to light but does not feed on nectar.

Place

Time   Date

Moth	Elephant hawk moth
Details	Pink and green, with a streamlined look. Visits honeysuckle for nectar.

Place

Time   Date

Moth	Angle-shades moth
Details	Wings look crumpled, like an autumn leaf: flies May to October.

Place

Time   Date

Moth	Brimstone moth
Details	Smaller and more yellow than swallow-tailed moth.

Place

Time   Date

Moth	Large yellow underwing
Details	Large; flashes yellow hindwings when it takes off; comes to nectar lures. Very common in late summer.

Place

Time   Date

Moth	Cinnabar moth
Details	Bright black and red pattern; comes to lights at night.

Place

Time   Date

TOP TIP

Moths like light. Try leaving an outside or porch light on after dark, and check for moths on lighted windows or walls. Most moths fly in the couple of hours after it first gets dark, so don't waste energy by leaving the light on all night.

DID YOU KNOW? There are more than 2400 species of moth in the UK, but only about 60 butterfly species. DID YOU KNOW?

Any others? Make a list in your nature diary, and take photos or make a sketch if you like.

Badger watch

We all know what a badger looks like. But have you ever actually seen one? Britain's favourite animal is hard to see, since it usually comes out only at night.

Visit a badger sett

You can watch wild badgers at their setts – the underground homes in which they spend the day. June is the best time to try. Contact your local Wildlife Trust group (www.wildlifetrusts.org) to see whether you can join a nearby badger watch. Or find out whether there is a badger sett near where you live and make a plan to visit with a grown-up who knows it well.

Finding a sett

Badger setts are usually on the edge of a wood, often in a bank or hillside – or in other wild places, such as old overgrown cemeteries. They have many entrances, so look out for several holes in the same area. These are bigger than rabbit holes and usually shaped like a capital letter D on its back. Also look out for badger trails, which look almost like narrow footpaths.

Is the sett in use?

You can tell by looking for:

- Fresh 'spoil heaps' – mounds of earth where badgers have been digging.
- Clear paths – if badger paths are covered with old leaves or plant growth you can bet no badgers have been here for a while.
- Scratching – badgers often leave scratches on tree trunks about 30 cm (12 in) above the ground.
- Badger hair (blackish with a white tip) caught on the bottom strand of a nearby barbed wire fence.
- Tracks – can often be found on badger paths after a wet night; look for five toes (not four like a dog or fox) and long claw marks.

What to do

1 Choose a warm, clear evening for your first visit. Plan to arrive half an hour before dusk. Wear warm, dark clothing and take a torch (plus spare batteries).

2 Approach the sett quietly and, if possible, from downwind (with the wind blowing towards you), so the badgers do not smell you. Don't go too close or use your torch when you are finding your place to watch, as this will scare the badgers off.

3 Find a comfy position with a good view of the sett, where you can sit quietly and won't need to move. Remember: you may be there for a long time.

4 Watch and listen.

With luck, badgers will appear as it gets dark. You may see their heads pop up from the sett entrance or hear them snuffling around in undergrowth nearby. Watch quietly and see what happens. With regular visits, you may get better views.

Low profile

Badgers may stay in their setts if they think people are around. Here's how to avoid detection:

🐾 **Don't be seen**
Wear dark clothing. Stay back from the sett, and don't sit against the skyline. Keep as still as possible.

🐾 **Don't be smelt**
Don't walk all around the sett and leave your scent. When watching, make sure any breeze is blowing from the sett towards you – not from you towards the sett.

🐾 **Don't be heard**
Avoid wearing clothes that rustle (a fleece is better than a waterproof). Don't talk or even whisper until after you have left. Don't make any sudden movements when pointing things out to one another.

Draw a badger

Badgers' stripy faces make them easy to identify. But they're not so easy to draw. That's partly because their real shape is hidden under all that fur.

Quick on the draw!

Here's how to draw a badger in five easy steps. You will need paper and a pencil. And coloured pencils, if you want to colour it in.

Step 1 ▶

Draw a longish oval for the body and, above it to the left, a smaller pear shape for the head. Tilt the pear upwards slightly – this will make the badger look livelier. Leave plenty of space for the neck: badgers have long necks under all that fur.

Step 2 ▶

Draw two smooth lines to link the head to the body. Use four more simple lines to show where the legs will go – these are a little longer than you may think.

Step 3 ▶

Draw around the body shape again and add the fur. The body fur comes halfway down the legs. Now complete the legs. The back feet are longer than the front feet and you can see claws on all the feet.

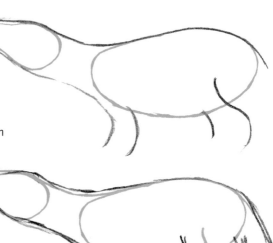

Step 4 ▶

Give your badger a face by adding an eye, nose and ears. Place the eye halfway between the nose and ear. A white dot near the top of the black eye will make it look shiny and alive. A small line will work for the nose. Don't worry about the mouth – you can't really see it at this angle.

Step 5 ▶

Draw two thick black stripes – one starting from just in front of each eye, and passing back through the eye and ear to join the dark body fur. The rest of the head is white, and the white fur extends a little way down the back and along the sides of the neck. Colour the body greyish-brown, with black legs and throat. Fine downward lines help show the furry coat. The tips of the ears are white.

Softly, softly

- ➲ Draw softly in pencil for steps 1–4. That way, once you're happy with the shape, you can rub out any lines you don't need.

- ➲ Get the shape right first; the colours and markings can follow later.

- ➲ Between each step, take a look at your drawing from across the room. Does the shape look right? If not, tweak it until you're happy. Always get the shape right first; the details can follow.

BIG STOAT

Badgers belong to the same family as stoats and weasels. They have a similar shape, with a long body and short legs, which is great for squeezing down holes. Badgers look fatter because of their thick fur, but really they are quite slim.

Wildlife window

Summer holidays can mean long journeys – and hours of travelling may not be your idea of fun. So why not use the time to do some wildlife watching?

Look out

A car or a train makes a great hide for spotting animals. You'd be amazed by how much there is to see – if you're quick. Here are some things you might spot.

Farmland birds

- 👁 **Rook:** like a crow, but usually in flocks; look for pale face and shaggy feathers around the legs, like trousers.
- 👁 **Lapwing:** flocks flash black and white in flight as they wheel around.
- 👁 **Pheasant:** male has bright colours and long tail.
- 👁 **Woodpigeon:** often flies dangerously low over the road.
- 👁 **Black-headed gull:** follows tractors in ploughed fields, searching for creepy-crawlies.

Birds of prey

On warm days, you can often see birds of prey flying in search of food.

- 👁 **Kestrel:** hovers on the spot – often above the edges of wide roads, where it catches mice and voles.
- 👁 **Buzzard:** soars on big broad wings above a wood or perches on a fence post.
- 👁 **Red kite:** once rare, but now easy to see in some areas; look for long, angled wings and a forked tail that keeps twisting.

Mammals

Mammals are harder to see (apart from farm animals, such as cows and sheep, which you can't miss). But here are some to look out for:

- 👁 **Rabbit:** the easiest mammal to spot; often nibbling grass on the verge.
- 👁 **Hare:** bigger than a rabbit, with longer ears; often in the middle of bare fields.
- 👁 **Roe deer:** often near the edge of a wood – sometimes in small groups.
- 👁 **Fox:** may trot across a field, usually in the evening or early morning.

Roe deer

Journey spotter bingo

Here's a fun journey game to pass the time. Every person on the journey gets a copy of the chart below (make your own simple version). Players win points each time they spot one of the animals on the chart. The first person to reach 100 points wins the game.

ROOK 10 points	HORSE 10 points	RABBIT 20 points
SHEEP 5 points	DEER 30 points	LAPWING 15 points
FOX 30 points	HERON 20 points	RED KITE 30 points
WOODPIGEON 10 points	MAGPIE 10 points	BADGER 50 points
COW 5 points	HARE 25 points	BARN OWL 50 points
KESTREL 20 points	BUZZARD 20 points	SWAN 15 points
PHEASANT 15 points	PIG 20 points	DOG 10 points

WARNING! Tell drivers that they do not get a score sheet as they should be keeping their eyes on the road. They can help the others if they like.

FLYING TO STAY STILL

FOCUS

You may wonder how a kestrel stays so still in the air. It hovers by flying into the wind at exactly the same speed that the wind blows it back – often using just tiny movements of its wings. So whenever you see a kestrel hovering you can tell which way the wind is blowing without even stopping to check.

Sea watch

You needn't travel around the world to see sharks, whales and dolphins. Lots of exciting sea creatures live around the UK coast. So keep your eyes peeled!

On the open wave

The best way to see marine wildlife is from a boat – maybe on a cruise or a ferry. Stay on deck and scan the sea for anything that breaks the surface. Be patient and you might see some of the following:

- **Seals** A shiny, grey blob sticking out of the water could well be a seal's head (see above). Use binoculars to see its dark eyes and long whiskers. Grey seals are larger than common seals, with a longer nose.

- **Basking shark** This giant fish feeds only on tiny plankton. Look out for two fins moving slowly along, three or four metres (10 to 13 feet) apart: the front floppy one is its dorsal fin; the back one is its tail. You can see basking sharks off the west coast.

- **Harbour porpoise** This small member of the dolphin family is the easiest one to see close to the coast. Look out for a low triangular dorsal fin turning over like a slow wheel as the porpoise arches its back through the water.

- **Dolphins** Bigger than porpoises, with a longer, more pointy dorsal fin. They swim fast and sometimes jump right out of the water. Bottlenose dolphins live near the coast; common dolphins live further out to sea.

- **Whales** The most common whale to visit Britain's coastal waters is the minke whale. Look out for its shiny grey back and small, hooked dorsal fin. This whale grows up to eight metres (26 feet) long – about the size of two cars. It does not often show its head or tail.

Bottlenose dolphin

Basking shark

Pointing it out

It can be hard to point out what you have just seen – especially if it disappears underwater. You can make it easier by pointing directly towards where you saw it and saying:

- whether it was moving to the left or the right
- where it was in relation to the horizon (e.g. 'Halfway between here and the horizon')
- where it was in relation to any other visible objects (e.g. 'Halfway between the lighthouse and that boat').

If you're facing forwards you could use the 'clock method'. Imagine that you are at the centre of a clock and the front of the boat is at 12 o'clock. Describe the direction of what you see as a point on the clock: e.g. a dolphin ahead and slightly to the left would be at about 10 o'clock.

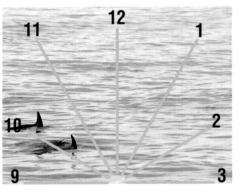

Tips for spotting ocean life

- Calm days are best. It is much easier to spot anything that comes to the surface when the sea is flat. Also you are less likely to be seasick.

- Take binoculars if you have them: sightings are often brief and far away.

- If you spot something come up briefly, scan ahead in the direction in which it was moving so you might see it when it next appears. Remember, dolphins and whales have to come to the surface to breathe.

AIR BREATHERS FOCUS

Dolphins and whales are mammals. Like all mammals (including us), they have warm blood and feed their young on milk. Unlike fish, dolphins and whales must come to the surface of the water to breathe air. Whales and dolphins belong to a group of animals called cetaceans. Over 25 different kinds have been recorded off the coast of the British Isles.

What's that fin?

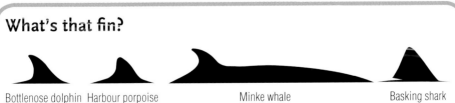

Bottlenose dolphin   Harbour porpoise   Minke whale   Basking shark

Make a sundial

Stuck indoors on a rainy day?
You could make a sundial for
when the sun comes out.
Sundials were telling the time
thousands of years before clocks.

Shadow clock

Sundials work because an object's shadow
moves as the sun moves across the sky
from east to west. A simple sundial
consists of two pieces:

❋ The **gnomon** (pronounced no-mon),
which sticks up to catch the sun's
shadow.

❋ The **dial plate**, which is where the
shadow falls.

DID YOU KNOW? DID YOU KNOW? The sun doesn't really move. It is the earth that moves around the sun, taking roughly 365 days (one year) to complete its circle. This journey is called an orbit. DID YOU KNOW? DID YOU KNOW?

To make your simple sundial you will need
these two pieces:

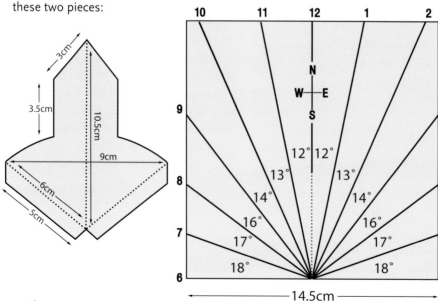

The gnomon

3cm
3.5cm
10.5cm
9cm
6cm
5cm

The dial plate

10   11   12   1   2

N
W — E
S

12° 12°
13°   13°
14°   14°
16°   16°
17°   17°
18°   18°

9   3
8   4
7   5
6   6

14.5cm

14.5cm

How to make it

You will need

Stiff card
Cardboard
Ruler
Protractor
Scissors
Pencil
Sellotape

❶ Draw the dial plate and gnomon on stiff card (one piece for each), following the measurements opposite. A ruler and protractor will help.

❷ Cut a slit into the dial plate along the red dotted line.

❸ Use closed scissors and a ruler to score along the dotted lines on the gnomon. Then fold along the lines as shown.

❹ Slide the folded gnomon into the slit in the dial plate and tape the flaps underneath.

❺ Stick the dial plate onto a sheet of cardboard to make it stronger.

How to use it

❶ Take your sundial outdoors on a sunny day and place it on a flat surface where it will catch the sun.

❷ Use a compass to find north. (Turn slowly in a circle until the pointer points north.)

❸ Position the sundial so that the north arrow points north.

❹ Where the shadow falls tells you the time. Check it against a watch – is it accurate?

TOP TIP

You can tell where north is by looking at a satellite dish. They always point south.

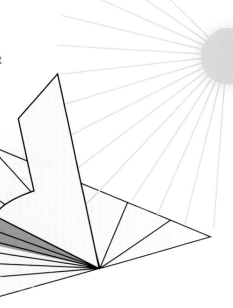

Your finished sundial

First flights

Look out for baby birds around your garden. Early summer is when they leave the nest and start to explore the world outside. They have to grow up fast.

Leaving home

Most garden birds set out once their feathers have grown enough for flying; a few, such as blackbirds, do it just before they can fly. They usually leave early in the morning, to avoid dangers such as hungry cats and sparrowhawks. Parents encourage them to leave by calling to them from outside.

Great tit feeding young

Baby birds that have left the nest are called fledglings. For the first few days their parents bring them food and look out for their safety. When you see blackbirds noisily scolding a cat you can guess that they have their young about.

To the rescue?

You may find a young bird sitting on the ground or hopping about. This is perfectly normal: it will take a day or two for it to learn to fly properly, and the parents are probably watching from nearby. It is best to leave it alone. If it is in an exposed place, such as on a busy path, you can move it somewhere safer. But always leave it close to where you found it, so its parents can find it, too.

Summer feeding

Keep your bird table and feeders stocked up during summer. If the weather turns bad – too wet or too dry – it can be hard for parents to find enough food to feed their young, so any extra you provide is a big help. The best things to put out are:
• black sunflower seeds
• fat
• fine oatmeal
• soaked sultanas, raisins
• mild grated cheese
• seed mixtures without peanuts
Important: Only put out peanuts in feeders with a very fine wire mesh, so the birds cannot remove big pieces that might choke their young.

How to spot a fledgling

Once a fledgling has left the nest it is usually as big as its parents and looks quite a lot like them. But there are several easy ways to spot that it is a youngster. Look out for its:

- fluffy, scruffy feathers
- short tail
- 'gape' – the colourful skin (usually yellow or pink) around a baby bird's bill that helps the parents see where to feed it

- begging – youngsters follow their parents around with their bill open and their wings trembling, begging for food
- high-pitched cheeping calls – also to beg for food.

DID YOU KNOW? Some birds, such as blackbirds, may raise two or more families per year, building a new nest each time. Each family is called a brood.

LOG IT Whose baby?

Some young birds have different plumage from their parents, which can make it hard to tell what they are. Can you identify each of the birds below and match the youngster with its adult? Mark in pencil first, just in case you change your mind!

①
②
③
④
⑤

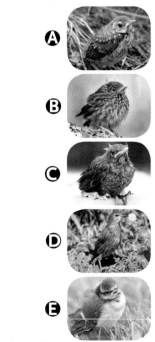

Ⓐ
Ⓑ
Ⓒ
Ⓓ
Ⓔ

Answers: 1: blackbird 2: song thrush 3: blue tit 4: starling 5: robin. 1-C, 2-A, 3-E, 4-D, 5-B.

Autumn

The countryside is changing colour: out go the lush greens, in come the fiery reds and yellows. Fallen leaves carpet the ground and fungi pop up all over the place overnight, thriving on the rotting plant matter.

But autumn also brings a feast. All kinds of animals fatten up on fruits before the hard times of winter set in. You too can enjoy wild food, such as blackberries. And why not have some fun with seeds, leaves and fungi while you're at it?

Keep a lookout for some special autumn animals. There are deer in the woods, spiders in the bushes and waders on the seashore. You can even learn some animal tricks, like getting camouflaged or making a survival shelter. Or give your garden a helping hand by building a compost heap.

Just turn the page for plenty of ways to enjoy autumn.

Berry delicious

Feeling peckish? Then grab a basket and go for a walk. In autumn there are fruits, nuts and berries everywhere. And the most delicious are blackberries.

Thorny fruit

Blackberries are the fruits of brambles. These thick, thorny bushes, with their long, twisting branches, grow in woodlands, hedgerows and waste ground. The fruits begin to ripen from August onward. They are food for all sorts of animals, from blackbirds to field mice – and, of course, for us!

Take your pick

Here's some good advice when picking blackberries.

- Wash blackberries thoroughly before eating them.
- Don't eat it unless you're sure it's a blackberry.
- Only pick the juicy black ones; the red or green ones are not ripe.
- Avoid bramble bushes beside main roads, industrial areas or fields that may have been sprayed with chemicals: the fruit may be polluted.

- Don't pick low-growing berries alongpaths popular with dog walkers. (Guess why!)
- Use a stick to help bring higher branches within reach.
- Careful of those wicked thorns: they can tear plastic bags – and your skin!
- Pick only as many as you think you'll need: remember, animals eat them too.

BRAMBLE SAFARI FOCUS

Red admiral

A bramble bush can be full of wildlife. You might spot spiders' webs between the stems or insects feeding on the fruit. Look out for fine squiggly lines on the leaves: these are made by leaf miners, the larvae of tiny moths, which leave little meandering tunnels as they nibble their way along.

More foods for free

There are more edible goodies you can look out for on your autumn walk.

Sweet chestnuts are delicious roasted over a fire or under the grill. You need to split each one with a knife so that it doesn't explode when heated. Get an adult to help you with this.

Rowan berries are scrumptious cooked with apples. They are best when picked in October.

Rosehips can be made into syrup, which tastes great on pancakes or diluted as a soft drink. They are full of vitamin C.

Rosehips

Brambles belong to the same family of plants as roses, called Rosaceae.

Recipe

Apple and blackberry sauce

Blackberries are delicious. And what's more they're packed with healthy vitamin C. You can eat them raw, or you can cook them to make jam, pies, tarts and other delicious desserts. Here's how to make apple and blackberry sauce, which will taste scrumptious with vanilla ice-cream.

Ingredients

450 g blackberries

1 large cooking apple, peeled, cored, and chopped into small pieces

115 g caster sugar

What to do

1. Wash all the fruit.
2. Measure out the right quantities and prepare the apples.
3. Put the apple and blackberries in a saucepan with a heavy base and cook for 20 minutes over a low heat.
4. Add the sugar gradually over the 20 minutes, stirring it into the mixture.
5. Stir every now and then to make sure it doesn't stick to the bottom.

Fun with fungi

Autumn is the season for fungi. Their weird shapes seem to pop up from nowhere, decorating lawns, logs and leaf litter.

Breaking it down

Fungi are called 'decomposers' because they get their nourishment from dead leaves and other rotting stuff. Even the furry mould that grows on old bread is a tiny fungus. When fungi break down something dead, all its nutrients – the good bits – return to the soil, helping plants to grow. So fungi are the best recyclers of all. Without them we would be up to our ears in rotting waste.

Fungi foraging

September and October are the best months to look for fungi. Different kinds grow in different places. Keep a note in your nature diary of what you find. Here are a few you might come across:

- **Birch bracket** grows on the trunks of birch trees; it has a tough, rubbery texture.
- **Fly agaric** looks just like a fairy-story mushroom, but it's poisonous; it grows underneath birch trees and pine trees.
- **Shaggy inkcap** has a tall frilly cap that quickly turns rotten and drips black 'ink'.
- **Puffballs** are white and round, like golf balls (though some grow as big as a football); they grow in fields.

Funky fungus facts

- The oldest fossil fungi are at least 545 million years old.
- Some fungi glow in the dark.
- Without fungi there would be no wine, beer or bread.

Below the surface

Mushrooms and toadstools are actually just the 'fruiting bodies' of fungus. The main part, called the mycelium, lies underground and consists of lots of tiny threads that spread in all directions to find food. The main job of a fruiting body is to release the tiny spores that develop into new fungi. Look under the cap of a mushroom: you'll see the gills, where these tiny spores grow.

Shaggy ink cap

LOG IT Make a spore print

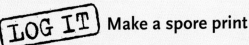

Spore prints are patterns left by fungi spores. This is how to make them:

❶ Collect a few different wild mushrooms in an open basket or paper bag. Choose ones with fully open caps. Use gloves and wash your hands afterwards.

❷ Remove the stalks from the caps.

❸ Place the cap gills-down on a piece of paper; use white paper for ones with dark spores and darker paper for ones with light spores.

❹ Cover the cap with an upside-down bowl to keep the moisture in.

❺ Leave it undisturbed overnight and return to look in the morning.

To display your prints, spray them with a clear fixative (hairspray works well) and allow them to dry.

TOP TIP

If you can't find any wild mushrooms, you can still do this activity with fresh open cup mushrooms from the shops.

Safety first

NEVER eat any wild mushroom unless a grown-up expert tells you it's safe. Some fungi are deadly. Always wash your hands after touching them.

Use this space to stick in your first spore print

Make yourself invisible

Looking for wildlife in the woods? Better make sure it doesn't see you first. Animals are experts at avoiding the attention of their enemies – or their prey.

Sneak up and blend in

To sneak up close to animals you need to copy what they do. Rule number one is stay hidden. Here are some tricks that might help.

1 Dress natural You don't need special camouflage gear. Just wear dull, natural colours, such as green and brown. Avoid anything bright, pale or shiny.

2 Skin deep Pale or shiny skin can give you away. You could smear some mud or soil for a more natural look. Blotches or stripes also help break up the telltale shape of your face. Wash your hands and face afterwards.

3 Stick to cover Use bushes or trees. You don't have to hide completely: branches or anything else that breaks up your outline will help.

4 Shading it Shadows are great for hiding in. But make sure that yours doesn't stick out and give you away. Remember: when you move, your shadow moves too.

The right moves

How you behave is just as important as what you look like.

- **Keep a low profile** Your upright, human shape is easy to recognise. So don't show it. Keep below the horizon as you approach.

- **Freeze** Animals spot movement very quickly. Learn to stay still. If an animal looks your way, freeze. No scratching or twitching – just make like a statue. If you find a comfortable spot in which to stay still, it may come closer to you.

- **Keep quiet** We humans are the noisiest animals on the planet. So watch where you walk. Put each foot down carefully, avoiding dry twigs and crunchy leaves. Use signs, rather than whispering. And don't even think about coughing or sneezing!

- **Not a sniff** Sorry to say this, but you stink! Animals can sniff us out in an instant. Avoid using scented soap. And don't bring smelly food. Standing in the smoke of a bonfire for a while can help disguise your human smells.

- **Not too close** You might scare the animal away. Once you have a really good view, just stay where you are and enjoy it.

Safety first

ALWAYS tell a grown-up where you have gone.

LOG IT

USE YOUR NATURE DIARY

Disappearing act

How invisible can you be? Hide yourself in a good spot in the woods and spend 20 minutes there without moving.

Tick the boxes if:

- an insect lands on you ☐
- a bird perches within five metres (17 feet) ☐
- a squirrel or other mammal approaches within five metres (17 feet) ☐
- you manage not to make a single noise in 20 minutes ☐
- a person walks past within ten metres (34 feet) without seeing you ☐

WHERE'S THE WOODCOCK?

FOCUS

The woodcock is a master of woodland disguise. Its colours and patterns look just like the leaf litter of the woodland floor. When danger approaches it stays still, knowing that it can't be spotted. That's why you hardly ever see woodcocks, even though they are quite common.

Build a survival shelter

Imagine that you're lost in the woods. It's getting cold and dark. And there might be bears around. What do you do?

Safe and dry

OK, so there are no bears in Britain anymore. But it's still good to know how to keep yourself warm, dry and safe. A simple survival shelter is quick and easy to make. And what's more, it's fun!

What to bring

Nothing. That's the whole point. You can build this shelter using just what you find.

What to do

Step 1 ▶

Choose a good spot. It should have lots of 'building material' nearby, such as sticks, branches and dead leaves. Try to find somewhere protected, like a natural hollow or under the low branches of a big tree. Avoid damp places, slopes and dead trees that might fall on your shelter. Also steer clear of clumps of nettles or an ants' nest.

Step 2 ▶

Find a sturdy branch 2–3 metres (6–9 feet) long. This is your ridgepole. Prop one end securely on a solid base, such as a rock or a tree stump, at about waist height. Or wedge it in the low branch of a tree, against the trunk. The other end of the ridgepole should be on the ground.

> **TOP TIP**
>
> **Protect the woods by using only old, dead sticks and leaves, not any part of a living plant.**

> **Safety first**
> ALWAYS tell a grown-up where you are and when you'll be back.

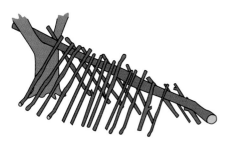

◀ Step 3

Collect plenty of smaller sticks. Prop these up along both sides of the ridgepole, with the longer sticks towards the raised end. Arrange the sticks so they leave enough room for you to get inside comfortably and are steep enough for rain to run off .

Step 4 ▶

Collect lots of thinner sticks and place them across and over the larger sticks. Weave them in and out where you can, to make a kind of lattice.

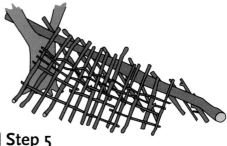

◀ Step 5

Gather pieces of bark, bracken and dead leaves. Arrange them over your shelter until you have built up a thick layer that covers it completely.

Step 6 ▶

Lay some more large sticks on top of the outer layer to stop it from blowing away.

Now you can crawl in and get comfortable. Nobody will even know you're there.

Finishing touches

- ◐ Keep your shelter small, low and snug. The bigger it is, the harder it is to keep warm inside.
- ◐ Don't use sticks or branches that are too heavy: you don't want the shelter to collapse and fall on top of you.
- ◐ Add a layer of dry leaves and/or pine needles inside to make a dry, comfortable floor.
- ◐ Keep a big leafy branch just outside – you can pull this into the entrance to seal it shut once you're inside.

Seeds on the move

Each seed that falls in autumn is a tiny starter pack for a new plant. Seeds can't walk, but they have some pretty smart ways of getting a ride.

Make a seed sock

Some seeds grab a free ride by sticking to the feet and fur of passing animals. They are then carried away to fall somewhere new – and, with luck, start growing. Seeds like this have tiny hooks that help them cling on. They can cling to your clothes, too. A seed sock shows how this works.

You will need

A pair of old fuzzy socks

Sterile, peat-free potting soil (from a garden centre)

10 small flower pots, or yoghurt pots with holes in the bottom

Water

❶ Pull the old socks over your shoes.

❷ Walk around in grass, sand, soil and old leaves. You could do this in your back garden or in the local park.

❸ Carefully remove the socks and take them home in a plastic bag.

❹ See if you can find any seeds stuck to the socks. How many can you identify? Use a plant book to help. Are any split open or beginning to sprout?

❺ Make a note of each seed in your nature diary, or do a drawing and give each one a number.

❻ Fill the flower pots with the soil – you need as many pots as you have seeds. Mark each pot with a number.

❼ Place the seeds in the soil, matching the number of the seed with the number on the flower pot.

❽ Water the soil every day. Watch what happens.

TOP TIP

If you don't find any seeds first time around, put on your seed socks again and walk somewhere else.

Dandelion parachutes

Pick the fluffy seed-head off a dandelion. Look closely: each piece of fluff is like a tiny parachute, carrying a seed. Count how many puffs it takes to blow away all the fluff.

Now try again, but this time, try to follow the seeds you blow away. Can you find any? How far did they travel?

Sycamore helicopters

The tiny wings on sycamore seeds make them spin when they fall. This keeps them in the air longer and gives the breeze a chance to blow them further away.

With a friend collect a handful of sycamore seeds. One of you drops them from a high place, such as your bedroom window. The other stands on the ground and tries to follow where they go. How far do they travel? Measure the distance by pacing it out.

Repeat the process and ask your friend to fan the seeds with a magazine to create a gentle breeze as they fall. Do they travel any further? Swap jobs and try it again.

LOG IT Sprouting success

Fill in the chart below to keep a record of how you get on with the seeds you have planted. Use your nature diary if you need more space.

USE YOUR NATURE DIARY

Type of seed	Date planted	Date germinated	Height after two weeks

Autumn leaves

In Autumn, leaves turn the ground into the ground into a carpet of yellows, oranges and reds. And there's plenty you can do with them.

Make a leaf headdress

Here's a great new look. It could even top off your Halloween costume.

You will need

Lots of dry leaves

Other autumn bits and pieces, like dry twigs and seed cases

A head band (Make this out of A strip of flexible card or craft paper, about 5cm wide and long enough to stretch around your head.)

A stapler, glue, Sellotape and scissors

❶ Pick the best leaves and lay them flat between the pages of a large book.

❷ Leave the leaves for about three days, until they are dry and flat.

❸ Stretch out the strip of card and arrange the leaves in an exciting design. Choose leaves that can stand up without drooping or tearing.

❹ Fasten the base of the leaves to the card. Use Sellotape or glue – whichever works best.

❺ Use scissors to snip off any bits that stick out where you don't want them.

❻ Strengthen your headdress by fixing some leaves together where they stick up above the card.

❼ Add the other interesting decorations you collected.

❽ Wrap the strip of card into a circle big enough to fit on your head and join the two ends together using the stapler or Sellotape. It should be neither too loose nor too tight.

Make leaf rubbings

What kind of leaves did you use for your headdress? You can keep a record of the best ones you found by making leaf prints. All you need is some thin paper and coloured crayons.

1 Pick the best leaves.

2 Place each leaf under a sheet of paper.

3 Colour lightly over the paper with a crayon, holding the leaf steady as you do so, until the whole of the leaf's shape shows through.

4 Now label the leaf – look it up in a book if you're not sure – and add the date and place you found it. See how many different kinds you can add to your collection.

TOP TIP

Add a mask to your headdress by fixing a couple of large leaves downwards over your face and carefully cutting eye-holes in them.

VANISHING GREENS

FOCUS

Leaves contain a chemical called chlorophyll that helps them make food for a tree. This gives leaves their green colour. But as winter approaches, the trees take a rest and live off the food they stored during the summer. The chlorophyll fades away, revealing the yellow and orange colours of the dying leaf.

Build a compost heap

Nature wastes nothing. Fungi and bacteria break down dead things and help more plants to grow. You can join in by building a compost heap.

Super soil supply

Compost makes richer soil for plants to grow in. And a compost heap is easy to build. You can do it in your garden – or ask your teacher if your class can build one at school.

A good compost heap has a mixture of material. 'Greens', such as grass clippings and weeds, are rich in nitrogen and rot quickly. 'Browns', such as cardboard and woody clippings, are rich in carbon and rot slowly. Together they create the perfect compost.

You will need

Lots of organic waste from your kitchen or garden (see the list below)

Four wooden posts, at least 50 cm (1.6 ft) high

8 wooden planks, each about 1 m (3.3 ft) long

Hammer and nails

Plastic sheeting or old carpet – at least 1 m² (3.3 ft²)

Four bricks

In or out?

Here are some things to add to your compost heap – and some things to avoid.

In

- Grass mowings: mix well with bigger items such as cardboard
- Garden clippings and trimmings: break big pieces into smaller bits
- Litter and droppings from small pets
- Kitchen waste, including raw vegetable peelings, egg shells and tea bags
- Egg boxes and toilet rolls – torn into pieces
- Dead leaves – but not too many at once

Out

- Meat/fish (may attract rats)
- Dog or cat droppings (disease)
- Coal ash
- Metal or glass
- Diseased plants
- Cooked rice, potatoes or pasta

What to do

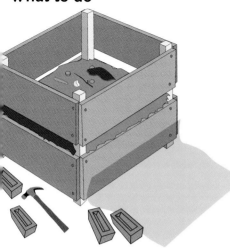

1. Find a site on soil or grass, where water can drain away and worms can enter from below. Choose an 'untidy' spot hidden from view.

2. Place the four corner posts in the ground one metre (3.3 feet) apart, to make a square.

3. Nail the planks to the posts (two on each side, as shown), leaving small gaps for ventilation. Ask a grown-up to help with this part.

4. Line the bottom with twigs and sticks.

5. Put in alternating layers of kitchen and garden waste, up to a height of at least 30 cm (12 in).

6. Secure the plastic sheeting on top with the bricks. This will keep in the heat and speed up the composting process.

7. Leave the compost heap alone – except to add more waste whenever you get a good load.

Safety first
Keep it clean! Always wear gloves when handling compost.

HOME IS A HEAP

FOCUS

Compost heaps can be wildlife havens. Reptiles and amphibians enjoy the warmth – grass snakes may even lay their eggs there – and hedgehogs find shelter too. When you spread out your compost the worms and many other mini-beasts will provide a feast for your garden birds.

Grass snake eggs and baby

8. Under the plastic sheet your waste should decompose (rot) nicely. Worms will mix it up while bacteria breaks it down. After a few months you should find a dark-brown, earthy layer at the bottom: perfect compost for your garden and pot plants.

Composting tips

- If your compost looks too dry add a little water.
- If it gets slimy and smelly add more dry stuff, such as straw or torn paper.
- If you don't have enough space for a compost heap, ask your parents or teacher to buy a compost bin. Local councils may supply these for free.

Draw a jay

For most of the year jays tend to hide away. But in autumn you can see these handsome birds out gathering acorns. Here's how to draw one.

Bird brains

The secret to drawing any bird is getting the shape right. You can do this by following these five easy steps. You will need paper, a pencil and a rubber – and coloured pencils, if you want to colour it in.

Step 1 ▶

Draw an oval for the body and, just above it, a small circle for the head. Leave a gap for the neck. Birds' necks can be hard to see beneath all those feathers, but they do have them.

Step 2 ▶

Draw two lines to link the head to the body. Add the tail – a jay has a medium-length tail, a little shorter than its body. Draw a smooth, rounded outline around the whole bird. Make the top of the head quite bulgy to show the jay's small crest.

Step 3 ▶

Add the jay's wing. A bird's wing makes a rough triangle shape when folded on the side of its body. Divide the wing into three sections, as in the picture: this shows where the different groups of feathers fall.

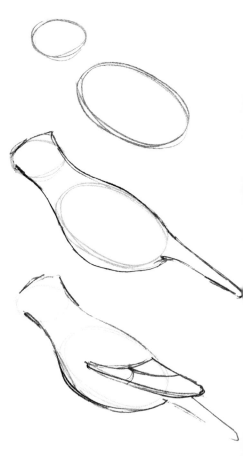

Step 4 ▶

Add an eye and a chunky beak. A bird's eye is always in line with the upper part of its beak. Also add the leg and foot, and a branch for the jay to perch on. You are seeing this jay from side-on, so only one of its legs and one of its eyes are visible.

Step 5 ▶

Add the colours and markings. A jay has a pinkish brown body, with white on the forehead, throat and under the tail. It also has a speckled forehead and a black 'moustache' sticking down beside its beak. The tail is black and the wings have neat markings in black, white and blue.

ACORN ANTICS **FOCUS**

Jays collect acorns in autumn and store them for winter food. They bury the acorns in secret hiding places, called caches, scattered over a wide area. One jay may bury more than 5,000 acorns each winter. It has such a good memory that it will find at least three-quarters of them. But many of the others remain undiscovered – and some may even grow into little oak trees.

Sketching sense

❧ Draw softly in pencil for steps 1–4. That way, once you're happy with the shape, you can rub out any lines you don't need.

❧ Get the shape right first; the colours and markings can follow later.

❧ Between each step, take a look at your drawing from across the room. Does the shape look right? If not, tweak it until you're happy.

Make a wind snake

Autumn can be a time of wind and rain and sometimes even big storms. Why not use your imagination and have some fun with the wind?

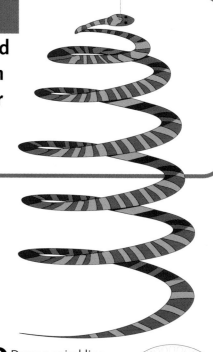

Serpent suprise

A wind snake is a good way to brighten up your autumn garden – and it's easy to make.

You will need

A paper plate

Markers, coloured pencils, paint or crayons

Scissors

String or ribbon

Stapler

DID YOU KNOW? Three kinds of snake are found in Britain: the adder, grass snake and smooth snake. None are found in Ireland.

Poison pattern

The adder is Britain's only poisonous snake. It is hard to see one in autumn, when snakes are preparing to hide away for the winter. You could copy its distinctive zigzag pattern to make your wind snake look like the real thing.

Adder

1 Draw a spiral line inwards from the edge of the paper plate. Leave space for the snake's head at the centre.

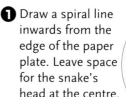

2 Colour the paper plate. You could make up your own exciting pattern – or you could make it look like a real snake (see the adder picture opposite).

3 Use the scissors to cut the paper plate along the line you have drawn.

4 Staple one end of the string to the middle part of the plate (the snake's head).

5 Now hang up your wind snake outside and watch it twirl in the wind. You could even make lots of them and have a whole army of twirling snakes in your garden.

 How windy?

How windy is it today? Is there a light breeze or a high wind? You can measure wind speed with a simple system called the Beaufort scale. All you have to do is watch what is happening outside and read the chart below. Check the weather every day for two weeks and fill in the chart.

Beaufort number	Wind speed	Description	What happens	Date recorded
0	0	Calm	Leaves don't move.	
1	1-5 kph (1-3 mph)	Light air	Leaves stir gently.	
2	6-11 kph (4-7 mph)	Light breeze	Feel wind on skin. Leaves rustling.	
3	12-19 kph (8-12 mph)	Gentle breeze	Leaves and smaller twigs moving.	
4	20-28 kph (13-18 mph)	Moderate breeze	Dust and loose paper blown up. Small branches moving.	
5	29-38 kph (19-24 mph)	Fresh breeze	Medium-sized branches moving. Small trees swaying.	
6	39-49 kph (25-31 mph)	Strong breeze	Large branches moving. Hard to use an umbrella.	
7	50-61 kph (32-38 mph)	High wind / moderate gale	Whole trees moving. Hard to walk against the wind.	
8	62-74 kph (39-46 mph)	Fresh gale	Twigs breaking from trees. Cars swerve on road.	
9	75-88 kph (47-54 mph)	Strong gale	Larger branches break off and some small trees blow over. Temporary road signs blow over. Damage to tents and canopies.	
10	89-102 kph (55-63 mph)	Storm	Trees are broken off or uprooted. Loose and damaged tiles peel off roofs.	
11	103-117 kph (64-72 mph)	Violent storm	Widespread vegetation d amage. Many tiles blown off roofs.	
12	118 kph or more (73+ mph)	Hurricane	Major damage to vegetation and some buildings. Objects may be hurled about.	

All at sea

The Beaufort scale was invented in 1805 by Sir Francis Beaufort, an Irish admiral. It was first designed to help sailors at sea, but in 1906 was adapted for use on land. Today people use many more modern methods, but the categories of wind speed remain roughly the same.

Estuary birds

No point going to the seaside when summer is over, right? Wrong! Autumn is great for coastal birds – especially where rivers meet the sea.

Chasing the tide

An estuary is a wide, shallow river mouth where a river spreads out into the sea. When the tide goes out it exposes lots of mud. This mud is packed with worms, crabs and other juicy titbits: all fantastic food for birds.

Many of the birds you will notice on the shore are waders. Most have long legs – for wading in shallow water – and many have long beaks, too. Thousands visit our coast every autumn. They have travelled south from where they nested. Some just stop off for a few weeks; others find so much food that they stay for the whole winter.

Watching waders

🐦 Use binoculars: the birds may be far away.

🐦 At low tide, waders spread out to feed. At high tide they gather on higher ground to rest. Visiting just before high tide is best.

🐦 Don't get too close and make them fly away: waders need to save all their energy for feeding.

🐦 Try to watch with the sun behind you so colours are easier to see.

🐦 Check their size, legs and beak to identify them. Bring a bird book to help.

Common waders

❶ **Curlew** Big, with a very long, curved beak; pokes deep into the mud.

❷ **Oystercatcher** Quite big; black and white, with an orange beak; feeds on mussels and other seafood.

❸ **Redshank** Medium-sized, with red legs; pokes in the mud; flies off noisily.

❹ **Ringed plover** Small with a short beak; black patterns on face and chest; runs in short bursts.

❺ **Dunlin** Small (sparrow-sized) with slightly curved beak; feeds busily in small groups, picking tiny creepy-crawlies from just below the mud.

Other estuary birds

Shelduck Big black-and-white duck with chestnut stripes.

Little egret Like a small, white heron.

Cormorant Big and black; dives under the water.

Shelduck

Safety first
Estuaries can be dangerous places. Dress to stay warm, and stick to the path. NEVER walk out on the mud.

EACH TO ITS OWN · FOCUS

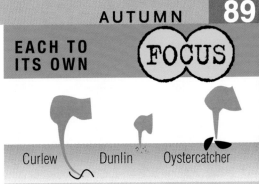
Curlew · Dunlin · Oystercatcher

Each wader has a beak that is suited to catching a particular meal. The curlew's long, curved beak can reach right down to lugworms that lie 10 cm (3 in) below the surface. The dunlin's shorter beak is very sensitive, so it can feel the movement of tiny creatures just below the surface and quickly grab them. The oystercatcher's beak is strong enough to smash open mussels.

LOG IT · Estuary bird log

USE YOUR NATURE DIARY

Keep a note in your nature diary of any birds you spot. Here are some to start you off.

Bird	How many?	Where?	When?
Curlew			
Oystercatcher			
Redshank			
Dunlin			
Ringed plover			
Shelduck			
Cormorant			
Little egret			

Deer oh deer!

You're out for an October walk when a terrifying roar echoes through the forest. Could it be an escaped lion? Do you dare get any closer?

In a rut

Don't worry. What you heard was probably a male red deer. In October red deer get together for the 'rut', when the biggest and strongest males (stags) round up a group of females (hinds) for mating. Each stag bellows out his roar to announce that he is the strongest. The sound can carry for miles.

Sometimes a stag has to chase away his rivals. They may even fight with their antlers. The winner mates with the females, who give birth to his young in the spring.

See the action

Find out the nearest place where red deer live and make a trip to watch the rut. Here are some things to look out for:

- Spot the stag. He's the one with antlers.
- What are the doing?
- Watch the stag. How does he behave towards the other deer?
- Look for vegetation caught in the stag's antlers. He often thrashes the undergrowth as part of his rutting display.
- How many females can you count?

DID YOU KNOW?
The red deer is Britain's largest land mammal. Stags can weigh up to 190 kg (420 lb).

TOP TIP

Some places run special guided walks to watch the rut. Find out on the Internet or try your local Wildlife Trust.

Safety first

Keep a safe distance – rutting stags can be aggressive. If you have a dog with you keep it on a lead.

Know your deer

The red deer is one of two species of deer native to Britain. The other is the much smaller roe deer, which has short antlers and does not live in herds. Four other species live wild in Britain, but these were all brought here from Asia. How many can you name? (Answers at the bottom.)

HEADGEAR

(FOCUS logo)

Only male deer have antlers. These are made of bone and have spiky branches, called points. Every spring they drop off and new ones grow in their place. Growing antlers are covered in a soft, sensitive skin called velvet. This peels away once they are fully formed.

Tracks and signs

Here's how to know when deer are about:

Tracks Deer have cloven hooves, a bit like sheep. Each foot leaves a distinctive track of two parallel slots – like the one above. Look out for them on muddy woodland paths.

Droppings Small, round and dark; often in small piles.

Tree trunks Bark may be rubbed (by horns) or nibbled (by teeth) about one metre (3.3ft) above the ground.

Twigs broken twigs with torn edges show where a deer has been nibbling.

Bedding spots A trampled hollow in the undergrowth shows where a deer has laid down for a rest.

Park life

Did you know there are red deer in London? Visit Richmond Park and you can watch the rut at close quarters. Other places in Britain to watch red deer include Exmoor, the New Forest, the Lake District, parts of East Anglia and the Highlands of Scotland.

Answers:
Fallow deer (pictured), sika deer, muntjac deer, Chinese water deer

Web designer

Look out early on an autumn morning for spiders' webs. You'll see them all over, strung among the grass and bushes, glittering with dew.

Sticky spirals

The female common garden spider builds a new web every day. It is neat and circular, with a spiral pattern in the middle. Look in the middle for her fat, pea-sized body with its white pattern. The web traps passing insects, such as wasps and flies. The spider rushes across to wrap up her victim in sticky silk, then she carries it back to the centre of the web and eats it.

How to make a web

You will need

A cork pinboard

A piece of card that fits onto the cork pinboard

A box of pins with round, coloured heads

Some fine cotton

A pair of scissors

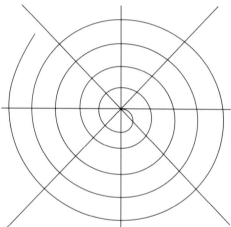

❶ Copy the design above onto the card, making it as big as you can. Start by dividing the square into eight, by drawing one cross through the middle and another cross from corner to corner. Start the spiral a little way in from one corner and wind it round into the middle.

❷ Stick your drawing to pinboard. Then stick in the pins: one at the end of each line and one in every place where two lines cross. You will need plenty of pins.

❸ Take a piece of cotton at least one metre long (3.3 feet long) and fix one end to any of the four corner pins.

4 Wind the cotton first around all the outer pins, then across the diagonals from one corner to another, and finally back across the middle to form the cross in the centre. Tie off the cotton around the final pin.

5 Take another piece of cotton for the spiral. Start at the outer end of the spiral and wind it into the centre, securing it around each pinhead as you go. Tie it off at the centre.

6 Use scissors to snip off any loose ends of cotton.

Hey presto! You now have a perfect spider's web – or at least something a bit like one. A real spider coats the spiral part of the web with a sticky liquid. This is what catches its prey.

DID YOU KNOW? In autumn, an area the size of one primary-school football pitch may contain five million spiders' webs.

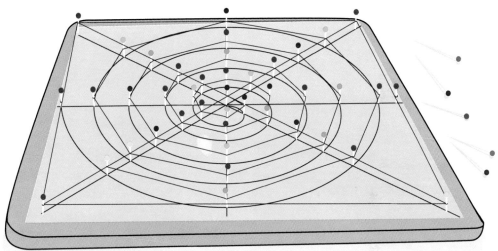

SILK ENGINEERS

FOCUS

A spider makes silk inside its body. It uses its legs to pull out the silk through tiny nozzles on its underside, called spinnerets, and keeps pulling out more as it moves along. One strand of spider silk is five times stronger than steel of the same thickness.

Hedgehog house

Do hedgehogs ever visit your garden? Perhaps they come at night, in secret. You can encourage them in by giving them a safe winter home.

Make it cosy

As autumn nights draw in, hedgehogs are looking for a safe, snug place in which to spend the winter. They collect leaves, grass, straw, bracken and other dry vegetation to build their own nests. For your hedgehog house you need to make something that looks and feels just like this.

❶ Choose a suitable site for your hedgehog home. It should be a quiet undisturbed spot, up against a bank, fence or hedge.

❷ Cut small air slits on each side of the box, and an entrance about 15 cm (6 in) wide in the front.

❸ Place the box in position upside down.

❹ Put some shredded newspapers and clean dry grass inside (but not too much, as hedgehogs prefer to gather their own bedding).

❺ Cover the top of the box with the plastic sheeting.

You will need

An old, sturdy cardboard box

A small piece of plastic sheeting (e.g. an old plastic bag)

Stones, earth, dry grass, twigs and leaves

Dry grass and/or shredded paper

Scissors

6 Pile twigs around and over the box to make a small dome, then cover this with dry grass, stones, earth and leaves until the box is hidden.

7 Now leave it alone. With luck, you'll attract a prickly visitor to spend winter in your garden. If it's a female, she may even have her babies there in spring.

DID YOU KNOW? A hedgehog is pale pink at birth with its spines still beneath the skin. Within hours the spines begin to grow through.

HIBERNATION (FOCUS)

Hedgehogs, get their energy from food such as slugs, and insects. But during winter this becomes harder to find. So they save energy by going into a kind of deep sleep, called hibernation. Their body temperature drops and their heartbeat and breathing slow down.

TOP TIP

For a ready-made hedgehog home you can use an old, upturned crate. Ask a grown-up to help you remove the inside partitions and cut an entrance.

Helpful hedgehog hints

- To avoid cold winter winds make sure the entrance does not face north or north-east. A south-facing entrance is best.
- Leave a supply of grass and twigs outside the entrance: the hedgehog may take this in as extra bedding.
- Clean the box out in spring. But first make sure there is no hedgehog still inside it.
- Always check compost heaps and piles of firewood before disturbing them, as hedgehogs may nest there.

Winter

Winter is hard for wildlife, with food and sunlight in short supply. Many plants take a rest from growing, while some animals hibernate to save energy. But nature doesn't come to a stop. Take a walk in the woods and you'll see buds furled up ready for spring. And there are plenty of tracks and other signs of animal activity.

Birds seem particularly busy, as they dash around trying to find enough food to keep them going. You can help by feeding them. Visit a bird reserve and you'll see just how many different kinds there are, including some that come to Britain only for winter.

Meanwhile we lucky humans can stay snug in our heated homes. But nature pays a price for all that energy we use. Find out how you can save energy by recycling – and have some fun at the same time.

Just turn the page for lots of winter ideas.

Go birdwatching

For a great winter's day out, try birdwatching. Nature reserves have loads of birds and lots of things that make birdwatching easier.

Wigeon

Whooper swan

Hen harrier

Winter water birds

The best reserves to visit are often those with some water, including marshes, lakes and estuaries. Here birds are easy to see and you can spot many different kinds – some of which have come to Britain especially for winter.

Ducks Males are generally more colourful than females. Look out for colourful wigeons, teals and shovelers.

Geese Wild geese arrive from the north in autumn and stay all winter. You might spot them in fields near water or flying overhead in noisy flocks.

Swans Bewick's and whooper swans arrive in winter. They have black-and-yellow beaks – unlike the orange beaks of our resident mute swans.

Waders Wading birds of many kinds gather in flocks around shallow water. Curlews are the biggest; they have long, curved beaks.

Birds of prey Birds of prey hunt over wetland areas in winter. Look out for hen harriers, peregrine falcons and short-eared owls (which fly by day). They may cause other birds to fly up in panic.

Reserve judgement

- Take binoculars and a bird book. Some reserves have binoculars for hire.
- Check opening times before you go. Some reserves are not open all the time.
- Never leave the path.
- Ask around: other people will be happy to tell you what they've seen and might have some good tips about what to look out for.
- Check the information centre to find out what's about and where to look. And don't forget to report any special sightings of your own.
- Allow plenty of time for sitting, watching and waiting – especially at hides.

Where to go?

The RSPB is one of several conservation organisations that manage nature reserves all over the country. Visit these websites to find a reserve near you.

RSPB **www.rspb.org.uk/reserves**

Wildlife Trusts **www.wildlifetrusts.org**

Wildfowl and Wetlands Trust **www.wwt.org.uk/visit**

Hide and seek

A hide is the perfect place for watching birds without them seeing you. Most hides have wooden seats and flaps that open up for viewing. Always approach carefully and enter quietly, to avoid scaring the birds. Then settle down and wait. If birds are not there at first, they will soon appear.

- Look everywhere: close to the hide, far off in the background and flying overhead.
- Open the viewing flaps slowly and carefully.
- Never stick anything out through the flaps: it could scare the birds away.

Start a list

Many birdwatchers keep lists of all the birds they see when they visit a reserve. Why not use your nature diary to do the same? You could note the species, how many you saw and what they were doing. You could even start a 'life list', noting down all the birds you have ever seen.

USE YOUR NATURE DIARY

Feed the birds

You don't have to visit a reserve to see birds. Try your garden. You'll be amazed by how many feathered visitors drop in if you feed them.

Where to feed

Feeding is not only fun, it also helps birds to survive. Extra supplies are especially welcome in winter when their natural food is scarce. Different species prefer different feeders, so provide food in a variety of ways to see the most.

On the ground

Scatter food onto your lawn or patio for birds that are ground feeders, such as starlings, chaffinches, blackbirds and thrushes. Don't put the food too close to any cover where pouncing cats might hide.

On the bird table

A bird table can be just a simple platform on a pole, with a raised rim to stop food falling off and gaps in the corners for drainage. Perfect for many kinds of bird.

On the feeder

Different feeders take different kinds of bird food, including seeds, peanuts and bird cakes. Hang them from a tree, a bird table or a pole. If you don't have a garden, try attaching a bird feeder to a window. You can buy ones with suckers that stick to the glass. Hanging feeders are good for tits and finches – and sometimes even great spotted woodpeckers (see below). Don't use mesh bags, which can trap birds' feet and beaks.

TOP TIP

Don't stop feeding once you've started: birds may come to depend upon your food, especially in bad weather.

Make your own bird cake

Make birds a special cake full of energy-rich foods. Soften some lard by warming it in your hands and then squash it together with a mix of seeds, nuts, dried fruit, oatmeal and grated cheese. Put the mixture onto a bird table or add it into a bird feeder.

What to feed

Different birds prefer different foods. Here are some to try:

From the shops

- Birdseed: mixed seed is good for all types; sunflower seeds – especially the black ones – are good for finches.
- Peanuts (hanging feeders): a favourite with tits, finches and woodpeckers.

From your kitchen

- Fat: suet, lard, bacon rind (chopped up small)
- Biscuit crumbs
- Cooked rice or potatoes (without salt)
- Cheese – mild and grated
- Old fruit – soft apples and pears
- Dry porridge oats

Greenfinches and robin

Tips for bird feeders

- Make your feeders easy to get at – for refilling and cleaning.
- If you buy bird food, get it from the RSPB, a pet shop or garden centre.
- Avoid salted foods: these are bad for birds.
- Keep a supply of clean water topped up (see page 104 for more on birdbaths).
- Clean your feeders and birdbaths regularly. Rinse with clean water, using gloves and a dilute disinfectant. Do it outside and wash your hands afterwards.

Keep watch

Once you start feeding, more and more birds will come to visit. So why not keep a regular watch and make a note of exactly what turns up?

Big Garden Birdwatch

Why don't you join the RSPB's Big Garden Birdwatch? This takes place every year on the last weekend in January. It's simple: just watch your garden for one hour and count the birds that you see, noting the highest number of each species that you see at any one time. (Don't count *all* the birds you see, otherwise you might end up counting the same robin ten times.)

Find out how to join by going to
www.rspb.org.uk/birdwatch/takepart

WELCOME KILLER

FOCUS

Sparrowhawks hunt garden birds. You may think this is cruel, but sparrowhawks need to eat too. They will not make your other birds disappear. In fact, a sparrowhawk in your neighbourhood is a sure sign that you have a good, healthy bird population.

Getting results

The Big Garden Birdwatch helps scientists to find out whether bird populations are rising or falling, and how factors such as climate change affect them. The ten most common birds recorded in gardens in 2008 were:
House sparrow
Starling
Blackbird
Blue tit
Chaffinch
Woodpigeon
Collared dove
Robin
Great tit
Goldfinch

1st

DID YOU KNOW? Britain has 15 million gardens. Together they take up more space than all our nature reserves put together.

Goldfinches made the Big Garden Birdwatch top ten for the first time in 2008. Finch populations are rising as winters become milder and they do not need to migrate to find food.

Goldfinch

LOG IT · Who eats what?

Use the table below to record which birds visit the feeders in your school or garden and what kind of food they are eating. Tick the box in the right places. If you see any birds that are not on this list you can record the results in your nature diary. You could also note other things, such as how the birds behave and how many there were of each kind.

	Peanuts	Birdseed	Bird cake	Fat	Fruit	Anything else?
Blackbird						
Robin						
Blue tit						
Great tit						
House sparrow						
Starling						
Chaffinch						
Collared dove						
Woodpigeon						
Magpie						

Baths for birds

Water is just as important as food. Garden birds need to drink regularly and keep their feathers clean. You can help them out with a birdbath.

Keep it shallow

There are many different ways to make a birdbath. A good one should not be too deep, and should have gently sloping sides so that any other creatures that tumble in can easily get out. Fill it with no more than 8 cm (3 in) of water. Here are two ideas:

Clay plant-pot saucer Set the saucer down on the ground or on top of an upturned clay pot.

Hanging pie dish If you don't have enough garden space for a birdbath on the ground, you could set a ceramic, deep-dish, pie plate inside a hanging basket and hang it from a branch. Some water will splash out so remember to refill it regularly.

Buy a birdbath You don't have to make a birdbath. You can buy all kinds of birdbaths, including some fancy, expensive ones. But birds won't care how much you spend, just so long as you give them clean, regular water.

Birdbath tips

🐦 Put in small rocks, or something else for birds to perch on.

🐦 The bottom needs a fairly rough surface to give the birds a solid footing. You could add gravel.

🐦 Place it somewhere out of reach of pouncing cats, but not too exposed. Birds often perch on nearby branches to scan for danger before they come to drink.

🐦 Raise it above ground to keep it safer from cats.

🐦 Clean it every couple of weeks using hot water, to keep the water clear and prevent disease spreading. Remember to wash your hands afterwards.

🐦 Top it up more often during summer – water evaporates quickly in hot weather.

🐦 In winter, keep it free of ice. Cold water thaws ice more quickly than hot water. (A floating tennis ball can also stop ice forming.)

LOG IT

Who wants a drink?

Use the table below to record which birds visit your birdbath. One example is included to start you off.

Species	Date	How many?
Blackbird	1 Dec	1

USE YOUR NATURE DIARY

A GOOD GULP

FOCUS

Watch how pigeons drinking at your birdbath spend longer with their heads down. They are the only British birds that can drink by sucking water up. Other birds have to take a sip then raise their heads to let the water trickle down their throat. Pigeons eat mostly dry grain and seeds, so they need a lot of water.

Make a nestbox

Do you have blue tits in your garden? Then why not put up a nest box for them? Better get cracking, so it's ready for the breeding season in early spring.

Boxing clever

Blue tits need a nest box with a small hole, just like the tree holes they use in the wild. You can buy one from the RSPB or other good suppliers. But it's cheaper to make your own – and more fun, too. Here's how:

You will need

One plank of wood: 150 cm (60 in) long, 15 cm (6 in) wide, and 1.5 cm (0.6 in) thick.

Pencil and ruler

25 nails (galvanised nails last longer) or woodscrews

Hammer – or a screwdriver if you're using woodscrews

Wire

Saw

A brace and bit

A piece of thick rubber, approx. 15 cm (6 in) by 10 cm (4 in) (from the inner tube of a bicycle tyre, for example)

A grown-up – to help with the tricky bits

Diagram measurements:
150mm (width)

- A (side): 250mm / 200mm
- B (side): 200mm / 250mm
- C (front): 200mm
- D (roof): 212mm
- E (base): 112mm
- F (back): 450mm

TOP TIP

Don't paint the box or use wood preservative. Artificial colours or smells might put the birds off.

❶ Use the ruler and pencil to mark out the plank of wood. Follow the above diagram *exactly*.

❷ Ask a grown-up to saw the plank into six separate parts along the lines marked in the diagram.

❸ Ask a grown-up to cut out the hole in piece C (the front) using the brace and bit. The hole should be 2.5 cm (1 in) wide and at least 12 cm (5 in) from the bottom.

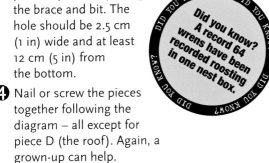

Did you know? A record 64 wrens have been recorded roosting in one nest box.

❹ Nail or screw the pieces together following the diagram – all except for piece D (the roof). Again, a grown-up can help.

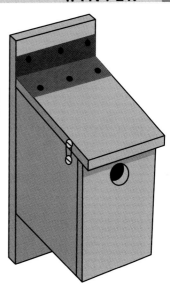

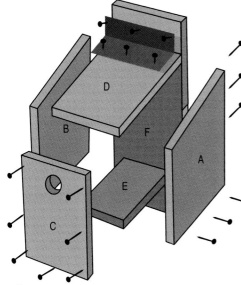

The hole truth

Other birds use bigger holes: great tits need them 2.8 cm wide; house sparrows and nuthatches need 3.2 cm (1.3 in) wide. Some birds, such as robins, prefer open-fronted boxes.

❺ Use the piece of rubber as the hinge for the roof: nail one side to the roof and the other side to the back of the box.

❻ Put in one screw on the roof and another on the side of the box near the top. Then make a catch from a piece of wire to keep the roof closed.

❼ Fix your nest box at least 2 metres (6.5 feet) high on a tree or wall, facing somewhere between north and east to protect it from bad weather. Do it before mid-February so it is ready for the start of the breeding season.

Nest box calendar

Looking after a nest box is a year-round job.

Spring If birds move in, leave them alone. Don't peep inside while the box is in use, but look out for youngsters making their first appearance.

Autumn Clean out the nest box when breeding is over (September onwards). Remove the nest and use boiling water to kill any bugs and germs.

Winter Once the box is clean and dry, add a small amount of clean hay or wood shavings. This may encourage mammals to hibernate in it – or birds to roost.

Winter gardening

The garden looks dead in winter. But it's still teeming with wildlife – and those dead plants still have important work to do.

Hideouts

Just because we can't see many animals in winter, it doesn't mean they've all gone. Many mini-beasts are hiding away, waiting for spring. These creatures are vital for keeping your garden healthy. Here's how you can help them:

Keep dead plants

Cracks and crevices are weatherproof winter homes for ladybirds, earwigs and lacewings. Dead plants also protect the soil and shelter other growing plants from frost, helping them to survive until spring. Besides, they make your borders look much prettier when they are covered in frost or snow.

Save the soil

If you clear away all your plant cover, the pounding rain will kill many small creatures, such as moth caterpillars and young spiders, that make their winter home in the soil. It will also make the soil too compact for worms and other creatures to do their important fertilising work so let some dead stuff stay.

Leave leaf litter

A good layer of old leaves protects the soil and allows worms and other mini-beasts underneath to keep making humus-rich soil right through the winter. Remember how the worms in your wormery mixed up the leaves you left on top? (See page 30.)

Blackbird

Piles of prunings

You could leave woody prunings lying out over winter. They provide a home for ground beetles, which kill slugs and weevils. A big pile might even shelter hibernating hedgehogs or slow-worms.

Seeds of survival

Many of the dead plants in your garden provide a feast for winter birds. Teasels last all winter long, and their seeds are favourites for goldfinches – as well as mice. By leaving old seed heads on plants, instead of 'deadheading' them, you will be helping many garden animals.

Welcome windfalls

Leave fallen fruit, too. Old apples and pears can be a lifeline for blackbirds, thrushes and starlings – especially when the winter gets very cold and there are no berries left on the bushes.

DID YOU KNOW? Spiders have a substance called glycol in their blood which prevents them from freezing to death – just like anti-freeze in a car. So they can keep hunting all winter.

HIBERNATING BUTTERFLY FOCUS

Some kinds of butterfly, including red admirals, peacocks and small tortoiseshells (above), hibernate in sheds, outhouses or even inside your house. Sometimes they wake up during warm spells. So if you find one flying around your house during winter don't let it outside. Instead place it in a well-ventilated box and leave it in a cool sheltered garage or shed. Check on it in early March.

Woodland wander

A winter wood can seem lifeless. The trees are bare, the birds are silent. It's as though nature has given up. But look closer.

Take a walk

Wrap up well and take a walk in the woods. Try visiting the same place that you went for your spring bird watch (see page 14) to see how different it is now. How many signs of life can you find?

Buds

New leaves and flowers are furled up inside buds on twigs and branches, ready to burst out in spring when it warms up.

Seeds

Acorns and other seeds scattered among the dead leaves on the ground may already be starting to grow.

Evergreens

Not all trees are bare. Evergreens such as holly and ivy keep their leaves all winter. Pine needles are really thin leaves. They lose less water than flat leaves, which helps pine trees to survive the winter.

TOP TIP

Listen. Winter is quiet. You may hear the rustle of a mouse or the call of a bird. Or you may hear nothing except the wind in the branches. Enjoy the silence.

Party birds

Blue tits, great tits and long-tailed tits often get together in small groups called 'feeding parties'. This helps them to find food. Look out for other birds that join them, such as goldcrests or treecreepers.

Robin song

Most birds fall silent in winter, waiting for spring before they start singing again. But robins keep going all year round. Listen out for their high, trickling song.

Squirrels

Winter is when grey squirrels get together for breeding. Watch them chasing each other among the bare branches – and look out for their untidy treetop nests, called dreys.

Tracks and signs

Animal tracks are easy to spot when it snows. And look out for other signs of winter animal activity, such as chewed pinecones or nibbled hazelnuts.

SQUIRREL SLEEPOVERS   FOCUS

Grey squirrels don't usually like other squirrels sharing their home. But on cold winter nights they sometimes relax the rules. Up to seven may cram into a nest built for one, helping each other to keep warm and snug. A squirrel will only allow in other squirrels it knows; strangers are turned away.

What's that tree?

Once trees lose their leaves it becomes harder to tell one kind from another. But there are still plenty of other clues to help you work it out.

Twigging it

Go for a walk in a wood where there are lots of deciduous trees – the ones that lose their leaves in winter. Take a closer look at the exposed twigs and buds and you'll see that each tree is different. Here are some common ones:

Ash Pale grey twigs with black conical buds set in opposite pairs and one big bud at the tip.

Beech Slender twigs with long, narrow, pointed brown buds.

Horse chestnut Dark brown twigs with large buds set in opposite pairs – apart from those at the tips.

Lime Shiny red zigzag-shaped twigs with buds arranged alternately.

Oak Clusters of buds towards the tip of each twig.

Sycamore Smooth grey twigs with bright green buds.

TOP TIP

Keep warm on your winter walk by wearing several layers. Warm air trapped between each layer keeps you from getting cold – and if you get too hot you can just take off the top layer.

Bark rubbings

Now the leaves have fallen it is easier to get a it is easier to look at a tree's trunk and branches. See how the bark is different on each kind of tree. Feel the trunk: is it rough and knobbly or smooth and shiny? Here's a fun way to make a picture of what you feel.

You will need

Thin paper – A4-size or larger

Masking tape

Thick crayons

A tree book – to help identify them

Big, mature trees

What to do

1 Choose a dry day to visit a place with a good variety of mature trees.

2 Find a tree, and tape the paper to its trunk at about eye level.

3 Gently rub the side of the crayon across the paper until the pattern of the bark shows. The ridges will show up darker than the hollows.

4 Write the name of the tree on the side or back of the paper, along with the date and place.

5 Repeat the process for as many trees as you can, until you run out of paper.

Compare your rubbings when you get home. Each tree has a unique pattern. You could stick them into a scrapbook or your nature diary.

Alternatively, you could stick them on the wall as decorations – or use them as wrapping paper.

TREE PROTECTOR

FOCUS

A tree has three layers of bark. The dead outer layer that we see protects the tree and prevents it from losing water. The cracks and ridges act as gutters to help rainwater run off the tree. Look closer and you'll find the bark also provides a home to spiders, earwigs (pictured) and many other tiny creatures.

Draw an oak tree

Drawing a tree is easy, right? Just a big lollipop of leaves stuck on a long brown stick. But drawing a *good* one is trickier. Here's how to do it properly.

Branch lines

The secret to drawing a tree is understanding its shape. That's why winter is a good time to start, when the leaves have fallen and you can see how the branches are arranged underneath. You will need paper and a pencil – and coloured pencils if you want to colour it in.

Step 1 ▶

Start with the outline of the whole tree. Draw a large circle with a flattish base that almost fills the page. Remember, an oak tree is as wide as it is tall. Then add the bottom part of the trunk. It is shorter than you might think.

◀ Step 2

Draw the main branches of the tree. They start to fork and divide low down (right at the base of your outline circle). Don't make them too even or symmetrical; each one should go off at its own crazy angles – and some twist behind others.

Step 3 ▶

Now add the thinner side branches. Take them right up to the edge of the outline circle. Each branch divides into other branches, each of which divides in turn. The branches get thinner as you move out towards the edges.

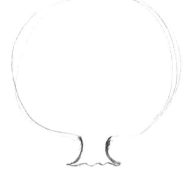

Step 4 ▶

Finally add the twigs at the ends of the branches. These are too small to see individually, so just shade with the side of your pencil to give the impression of lots of little twigs. If you're using colour, shade the trunk and branches.

You could turn your winter tree into a summer tree by adding leaves. Just cut out a piece of green paper to fit exactly over your original outline. Give it a nice clumpy edge and cut a few holes so you can see through. Use Magic Tape to stick it down, so you can remove it and show the branches underneath.

Shaping up

No two trees look the same. Every species has its own distinctive shape, and each individual tree differs from the next, depending upon what kind of soil it grows in and how much light it gets. An oak tree in dense woodland grows taller and thinner than one in the middle of a field.

DID YOU KNOW? There are more than 400 different kinds of oak tree worldwide.

Here are the shapes of three common trees: beech, silver birch and hazel. Can you tell which is which? Answers at the bottom.

❶

❷

❸

Answers: 1. silver birch 2. hazel 3. beech

Plaster prints

Wild animals can be hard to spot. But their tracks tell you when they've been around. Here's a great way to keep a record of who trod where.

Track them down

Look for tracks beside water, around muddy fields or on damp sand. Go on a dry day, soon after it has rained. And set out early, before the tracks are spoiled.

You will need

Container of Plaster of Paris

Plastic bottle of water (sea water is fine on the beach)

Cardboard strips, about 8 cm (3 in) wide by 30 cm (12 in) long

Plastic mixing bowl

Plastic mixing spoon

Newspaper

❸ Use a spoon to mix two parts Plaster of Paris with one part water in the mixing bowl. It should become thick and creamy, like pancake batter. Stir until all the lumps are gone. Be sure you mix enough to do the job.

❹ Gently spoon the plaster into the track. Make sure you fill in all details. Do not let it overflow the cardboard.

What to do

❶ Find a clear animal track and carefully remove any loose leaves or sticks.

❷ Make a low wall around the track with the cardboard strip. Tape the ends together and press it gently into the soil so no plaster will run away.

5 Wait for the plaster to harden. This can take 30 minutes to one hour, depending on how wet the ground is. Once the Plaster of Paris feels dry, tap it gently with your knuckles. If it sounds hard, then it is safe to pick up.

6 Lift the cast straight up. You may need to dig out some of the soil from underneath first, but do not pry with a stick. Carefully dust off any dirt and remove the cardboard ring.

7 Pack your cast carefully in newspaper and take it home.

8 Allow it to dry for several days before cleaning it or painting it.

Care for your casts

- Never wrap plaster casts in plastic bags – this prevents moisture getting out.
- Clean your cast by holding it under running water and gently rubbing away excess dirt.
- Out-of-date Plaster of Paris may not set properly.
- Never leave your cast soaking in water: it will start to soften.
- If you paint your cast, leave one surface unpainted so moisture can escape.

More signs

Look out for other signs animals leave behind:

Hair on the bottom of a fence where a badger has wriggled underneath

Hazelnut shells: split in two means a squirrel; neat hole means a mouse or vole

Pine cones stripped by a squirrel

Who is it?

Can you identify what animal made the print in your cast? Look to see whether it has hooves, like a deer, or pads and toes, like a fox. Look for claw marks (cat tracks don't show claws) and count the toes. A book on tracks will help. Here are some you might find.

Fox Like a dog, but longer and thinner.

Badger Five toes and long claws.

Rabbit Back foot (right) bigger than front foot (left).

Squirrel Small, with tiny fingers.

Roe deer A neat shield split in half.

Flocking together

Ever noticed how some birds form flocks during winter? You might see hundreds perched together or flying overhead. But what are the up to?

Birds of a feather

Joining a flock helps birds to survive. It gives them more eyes to spot danger and more voices to sound the alarm. Also, a predator – such as a bird of prey – finds it hard to pick out one victim when there are so many to choose from. Flocks often form late in the day: the birds roost together overnight then set out in their own directions the next morning.

Starlings

Three to look out for

Starlings flock to their evening roosts in huge numbers. Tens of thousands may gather in city centres, reedbeds and old piers. Watch them swirl around in the air. They fly so close together that from a distance they look like smoke.

Gulls come inland during winter to gather on rubbish tips and playing fields. Watch them fly overhead back to their roosts every evening in long, wavy lines.

Ducks gather on lakes and reservoirs during winter. They roost on the water, where they are safe from any danger on the bank.

WINTER WANDERERS

FOCUS

Fieldfares are among many birds that breed in northern countries but visit Britain to spend the winter. Here they find a milder climate and more food. Even many common 'British' birds, including starlings, lapwings and chaffinches, are joined by thousands of their own kind from overseas. This explains why flocks of these species can become so big in winter.

Counting birds

Flocks of birds are hard to count, especially when flying, so you will never get a completely accurate number. But you can make a good estimate by counting part of the flock then multiplying it. For instance, if you count 20 birds, and the flock looks about five times bigger than the bit you counted, your estimate is 120 birds. The picture here gives you an idea.

Other winter flockers

Pied wagtail towns and car parks
Chaffinch woods
Lapwing fields
Woodpigeon woods and fields
Geese coastal fields

14 birds

LOG IT How many?

Look out for flocks of the following birds and record the highest number you see at any one time. Note the date and place. We've filled in one to get you started. Use your nature diary if you need more space.

Bird	How many?	Where?	When?	Comments
Lapwing	±220	Field behind school	5 Dec	All sitting facing into the wind
Starling				
Wild geese				
Coot				
Chaffinch				
Pied wagtail				
Rook				

Saving energy

As winter gets colder we use more energy to keep warm. But burning energy speeds up global warming around the world. So what should we do?

Making a difference

There are many simple ways to save energy at home. You might think there's no point, when big polluters, such as aircraft and factories, cause so much more pollution than us. But small changes make a big difference if enough people join in. Here are some to get you started:

Buy locally produced food Most supermarket food has travelled a long way, which burns more energy and causes more pollution.

Turn off lights Don't forget to switch lights off when you're not using them.

Fit energy-efficient light bulbs Don't leave TVs and other appliances on standby.

Recycle waste Glass, cans, paper and cardboard all cost energy to produce. Try to re-use whatever you can – and recycle containers and packaging. Reducing waste helps protect wild places and wildlife.

Compost food waste Use it in your garden (see page 82 for details).

Save water Fit low-flow showerheads and a low-flush toilet; only use the dishwasher when full. It costs lots of energy to supply, treat and heat water. Saving water helps protect our rivers and wetlands for wildlife.

Insulate your home Seal gaps and cracks to save energy and lower your heating bill.

Leave the car at home Cars can produce nearly half one family's greenhouse gas emissions. Instead, share someone else's car, take a bus, walk or cycle.

Some of these things need a grown-up's help; others you can do by yourself. For more ideas and advice see **www.rspb.org.uk/advice/green/index.asp**

Calculating carbon

Your 'carbon footprint' describes how much impact you make on the planet due to the CO_2 that you produce. Everybody has one. You can measure yours by working out how much energy you use every day. Try to answer the following questions (ask a grown-up if you need help).

1 How much gas do you use on average per month? (Divide your monthly household gas bill by the number of people who live in your house.)

2 How much electricity do you use on average per month? (Divide your monthly household electricity bill by the number of people who live in your house.)

3 If you use a car at home, how far does it drive you on average every month? (Ask the car driver the total mileage for that month and divide it by the number of people in your house who use the car.)

4 Do you get to school by car, bus, bicycle or walking?

5 You can use all of this information to calculate your personal CO_2 emissions. Visit a carbon footprint calculator on the web (**www. carbonfootprint.com**) and try it for yourself. You'll be amazed at how much carbon you use – and how much you could save.

DID YOU KNOW? One third of water used in the average UK household goes down the toilet.

WARMING UP

FOCUS

The earth stays warm because gases in the atmosphere, called 'greenhouse gases', trap heat from the sun. This is natural: without it, the earth would be too cold for life to survive. But people today are producing too many extra greenhouse gases – especially carbon dioxide (CO_2) – and this affects our climate.

CO_2 is stored in 'fossil fuels', such as oil and coal, which formed when dead plants became buried millions of years ago. By burning these fuels in our vehicles, offices and homes we release more CO_2 into the atmosphere.

Make your own paper

Here's some recycling you can do all by yourself. It's a great way to reuse old paper. It saves trees, it saves money and – what's more – it's fun!

Recycling trees

Paper is made from cellulose – the plant fibres that come from trees. By recycling paper you can use those same fibres over and over again. Here's how:

You will need

Old food processor or blender

Iron and ironing board

Old wire coat hanger

Old pair of tights

Newspaper or other paper

White glue

Water

Big sink or tub filled with 10 cm (4 in) of water

Pack of J-cloths

Soft towels

Plenty of space (you're going to make a big mess!)

1 Tear up the newspaper into small squares of no more than 5 cm (2 in) and soak them in warm water for a few hours (overnight, if possible).

2 Bend the coat hanger into a square or rectangle to make a frame. Stretch one leg of the tights over the frame, keeping it pulled tight and flat.

3 Put a handful of the torn-up paper and some water into the food processor or blender. Get a grown-up to help with the blending. Blend the mixture on high until it becomes like thick soup. Keep adding more paper and water until the blender is full. Run it until the paper is no longer visible – then continue for two more minutes.

4 Pour the paper pulp into the sink water and add two tablespoons of white glue. Mix it up really well using your hands.

5 Lower the frame carefully to the bottom of the sink, then lift it out very slowly while counting to ten. Hold it over the sink for two minutes, letting the water drain out.

6 Turn the frame gently over onto a J-cloth, with a folded towel underneath to absorb the water. Then remove the frame gently, leaving your square of paper pulp on the cloth. Put another J-cloth on top.

7 Iron your piece of paper with the J-cloths still on, then hang it up to dry. Ask an adult to help with the ironing.

8 Keep making paper until the pulp is all strained out of the sink. Stir the mixture every time you make a new piece.

9 Once your paper is completely dry, peel it gently off the cloth. Hey presto! You should now have a sheet of your own homemade, recycled paper.

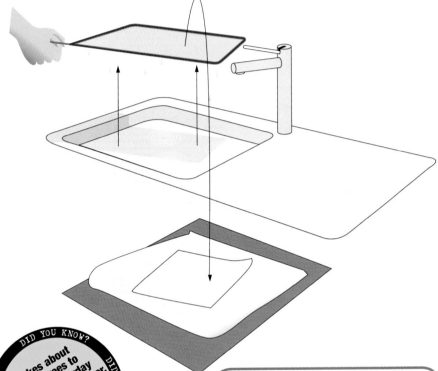

DID YOU KNOW?
It takes about 20,000 trees to make the Saturday edition of a newspaper. That's more than one million trees a year.

Write a letter

Now you're ready to write something on your paper. If you feel strongly about recycling and saving energy, you could write a letter to your MP, telling him or her your views. MPs can only help change things if they know what people think. Explain that you made the paper yourself; this will show that you're serious.

You can find out the name and address of your MP by logging onto **www.theyworkforyou.com** and entering your postcode.

TOP TIP

Make your paper more colourful by mixing onion skins into the blender. Or add some leaves for a more interesting texture – do this once you've removed the frame from the water but before you've pressed it.

Glossary

Amphibian Animal, such as frog, toad or newt, that has smooth, moist skin and lays its eggs in water

Antennae 'Feelers' on the head of an insect that it uses to sense things

Aphid Small insect belonging to the bug family, sometimes called greenfly

Atmosphere Blanket of gases that surrounds the earth and includes the air that we breathe

Bird of prey Bird, such as a hawk or eagle, that kills and eats other animals

Brace and bit Hard tool used to drill holes in wood

Breeding season Time of year when animals have their young

Brood Family of young birds in a nest

Camouflage Colours or patterns that help something to hide by blending into its background

Carbon dioxide (CO₂) Gas that animals breathe out and plants breathe in; it is also produced by burning fuel and causes pollution in the atmosphere

Catkin Small cluster of tiny flowers that hangs from trees such as willow, birch and hazel

Cast Piece of Plaster of Paris that has set solid around something

Ceramic Made of pottery or china

Climate change Gradual change in the pattern of the Earth's weather

Colony Group of animals living together

Dawn chorus Many birds singing together at daybreak, mainly in spring

Deadhead Remove the dead flowers or seed heads of plants

Decompose Rot and break down

Dorsal fin Single fin on the back of most fish, whales and dolphins

Downwind In a position where the wind is coming towards you

Estuary Shallow coastal bay where a river meets the sea

Fertiliser Substance spread on soil to help plants grow

Fledgling Young bird that has just left the nest and is learning to fly

Fruiting body Fleshy, visible part of a fungus, such as a mushroom or toadstool

Fungi Group of plant-like living things that comprises mushrooms, toadstools and their relatives

Germinate Sprout from a seed and start growing

Gills Organs through which fish and some other creatures breathe air underwater.

Global warming Gradual rise in the earth's average temperature

Habitat Place or landscape in which a creature naturally lives; can be small, like a pond, or big, like a mountain

Hibernation Long period of rest that some animals take during winter, during which their body processes slow down in order to save energy

Hide Small building from which to watch wildlife without it seeing you

Horizon line in the far distance where the earth and sky seem to meet

Humus Decomposed matter in the soil that enriches it and helps plants to grow

Insulate Cover or wrap something up to prevent it losing heat

Invertebrate Animal without a backbone, including insects, spiders, slugs, crabs and other mini-beasts

Lattice Criss-cross structure

Larvae young of insects and some other mini-beasts; caterpillars are the larvae of butterflies and moths

Lichen Primitive plant that grows like a crust on walls, branches and other surfaces

Lure Bait put out to attract something

Mammal Warm-blooded animal, such as dog, mouse or human, that suckles its young on milk; most mammals are furry and give birth to live young

Marine Living in the sea

Migration Seasonal journey that some animals make in order to find food

Mini-beast Popular name for insects and other invertebrates

Mouthparts The parts of an insect or other invertebrate that it uses for eating

Nectar Sweet, syrupy liquid produced by plants

Nourishment Goodness from food

Nutrient Healthy part of food; good food contains many nutrients

Nymph Young form of some insects, such as dragonfly and mayfly

Orbit Regular journey that one object makes around another, such as the earth around the sun

Plankton Microscopic animals and plants that float in water

Plumage All the feathers of a bird

Reptile Animal, such as snake, lizard or tortoise, that has dry scaly skin

Resident Always living in the same place

Roost Gathering of birds for sleep or rest

Scrub Overgrown wasteland with thick bushes and small trees

Species single, unique type of animal that cannot breed successfully with any other type

Topsoil Surface layer of soil that contains most of the goodness that plants need to grow

Trellis Wooden criss-cross structure on which climbing plants can grow

Wader Bird with long legs, such as curlew, that wades in shallow water to find food

Woody Describes the tough, fibrous parts of plants, such as roots and branches

Useful information

The RSPB speaks out for birds and wildlife, tackling the problems that threaten our environment. Nature is amazing – help us keep it that way. Find out more at: **www.rspb.org.uk**

Find out more about RSPB Wildlife Explorers and how to become a member at: **www.rspb.org.uk/youth**

Other websites

Big Garden Birdwatch
www.rspb.org.uk/birdwatch

The Wildlife Trusts (including Wildlife Watch) **www.wildlifetrusts.org.uk**

BBC Science and Nature (including Springwatch, Autumnwatch and advice on garden wildlife)
www.bbc.co.uk/nature/animals/wildbritain

Wildfowl and Wetlands Trust
www.wwt.org.uk

British Butterfly Conservation
www.butterfly-conservation.org

UK Moths **www.ukmoths.org.uk**

Wildlife Britain **www.wildlifebritain.com**

Wildlife Gardener
www.wildlifegardener.co.uk

UK Department of the Environment (lots of information and activities to do with climate change) **www.defra.gov.uk/schools**

WWF UK (information on wildlife and conservation at home and around the world) **www.wwf.org.uk**

Books

RSPB Children's Guide to Birdwatching, Mike Unwin and David Chandler, A&C Black, 2005

All about Garden Wildlife, David Chandler, New Holland, 2008

RSPB Handbook of Garden Wildlife, Peter Holden and Geoffrey Abbot, Christopher Helm, 2008

Collin's Gem Garden Wildlife, Michael Chinery, Collins, 2006

Nature's Calendar, Chris Packham, Collins, 2007

Nick Baker's Bug Book, Nick Baker, New Holland, 2002

Nick Baker's British Wildlife: A Month by Month Guide, Nick Baker, New Holland, 2006

Index

Acknowledgements

Pages: 2 IStockphoto/Andrew Howe, IStockphoto/Chris Hepburn, IStockphoto/Chris Crafter, IStockphoto/Lukasz Kulicki, IStockphoto/Andrew Howe; 3 Kathy Gemmell; 4 IStockphoto/Maurice van der Velden, IStockphoto/Paula Connelly; 5 IStockphoto/pixhook, IStockphoto/Andrew Howe; 6 IStockphoto/Maurice van der Velden, IStockphoto/Andrew Howe, IStockphoto/Anna Yu, IStockphoto, Phil Morley, IStockphoto/Tim Walton, IStockphoto/Adrian Assalve, IStockphoto/Andrew Howe, IStockphoto/Robert Ellis, David Tipling (rspb-images.com); 7 IStockphoto/Sven Peter, IStockphoto/assalve, IStockphoto/Ken Hewitt, IStockphoto/George Clerk, IStockphoto/Andy Gehrig, IStockphoto/Bruce Block, IStockphoto/Gary Martin, IStockphoto/ kevin kane; 9 Mike Unwin 10 Peter Gates, IStockphoto/Chris Hepburn, IStockphoto/Andrew Howe, Peter Gates; 11 Peter Gates, Marvin Dembinsky Photo Associates / Alamy, Peter Gates, Stockphoto/Merlin Farwell, Chris Gomersall (rspb-images.com), IStockphoto/Andrew Howe, IStockphoto/Anna Yu; 12 IStockphoto/Anna Yu, IStockphoto/Sven Peter, IStockphoto/ Andrew Howe; 14 IStockphoto/Andrew Howe, Chris Gomersall (rspb-images.com); 15 IStockphoto/Andrew Howe; 16 Peter Gates, IStockphoto/Maurice van der Velden; 18 IStockphoto/Marianne Fitzgerald; 19 Peter Gates; 20 Marvin Dembinsky Photo Associates / Alamy, Wildchromes / Alamy; 22 IStockphoto/Alasdair Thomson; 23 Ray Kennedy (rspb-images.com), IStockphoto/Robert Ellis; 24 IStockphoto/Chris Hepburn; 25 IStockphoto/Laurie Knight; 26 Mike Lane (rspb-images.com), Andrew Parkinson (rspb-images.com); 27 Bob Glover (rspb-images.com); 28 IStockphoto/Joe Gough; 30 Peter Gates, Erica Olsen/FLPA; 32 IStockphoto/ Andrew Howe, IStockphoto/Živa Kirn, Terry Whittaker/FLPA; IStockphoto/Pavel Lebedinsky; 33 IStockphoto/Merlin Farwell, IStockphoto/Tom Hermansson Snickars; 34 Richard Revels (rspb-images.com); 36 Peter Gates, IStockphoto, IStockphoto/ Giorgio Perbellini, IStockphoto/George Clerk, IStockphoto/ Giorgio Perbellini, IStockphoto/Paula Connelly, Peter Gates, IStockphoto/Eric Shaw, IStockphoto/Joze Pojbic, IStockphoto/ Chris Crafter, 37 Peter Gates, IStockphoto/Andrew Howe, IStockphoto/Jim DeLillo, IStockphoto/Giorgio Perbellini, IStockphoto/Alasdair Thomson; 38 IStockphoto, Phil Morley / Alamy, IStockphoto/Tim Walton, Shutterstock/klausenstein, IStockphoto/Gary Martin; 39 IStockphoto/ kevin kane, Manor Photography / Alamy, blickwinkel / Alamy, Michael Vitti / Alamy ; 41 IStockphoto/Joze Pojbic; 42 IStockphoto/Gianluca Padovani, IStockphoto/Andrew Howe; 43 IStockphoto/Alasdair Thomson, Andrew Harrington / Alamy; 44 IStockphoto, IStockphoto/ Eric Shaw, IStockphoto, IStockphoto/Giorgio Perbellini; 46 IStockphoto/Alasdair Thomson; 48 Iain Davidson Photographic / Alamy, IStockphoto/Paula Connelly, IStockphoto/Ian Murdie, IStockphoto, IStockphoto/Willi Schmitz, Peter Gates; 49 IStockphoto/Sergey Chushkin; 50 IStockphoto/Rebecca Grabill, IStockphoto/Eric Forehand; 52 IStockphoto/Jim DeLillo, IStockphoto/Simon Smith, Peter Gates, IStockphoto; 53 1Apix / Alamy; 54 Rolf Nussbaumer / Alamy, IStockphoto/Serdar Yagci, IStockphoto/john anderson; 55 Michael Menzlaff, IStockphoto/ Gertjan Hooijer, www.nature-shetland.co.uk, Jeffdelonge, www. nature-shetland.co.uk, IStockphoto/Laurie Knight;

56 IStockphoto/Lauri Wiberg, IStockphoto/Kurt Hahn; 57 Papilio / Alamy; 58 IStockphoto/Chris Crafter; 59 IStockphoto/jlj_images; 60 IStockphoto, IStockphoto/ Giorgio Perbellini; 61 Mark Hamblin (rspb-images.com); 62 IStockphoto/Anna Yu, IStockphoto/George Clerk, Chris Gomersall (rspb-images.com); 63 IStockphoto/George Clerk; 64 IStockphoto/Mark Goddard; 66 IStockphoto/Ken Hewitt; 67 IStockphoto/Andrew Howe, IStockphoto/Stephen Rees, IStockphoto/Andrew Howe, IStockphoto/Lee Pettet, IStockphoto/Andrew Howe, IStockphoto/hazel proudlove, IStockphoto/Ola Moen, IStockphoto/Ken Hewitt, IStockphoto/ Dmitry Maslov, IStockphoto/Maurice van der Velden; 68 Peter Gates, IStockphoto/Lukasz Kulicki, Peter Gates, IStockphoto/ Karel Broz, IStockphoto/Andy Gehrig, IStockphoto/Adrian Assalve, IStockphoto/Andrew Howe; 69 Mark Boulton / Alamy, IStockphoto/Maxim Filipchuk: 70 IStockphoto/Adrian Assalve, IStockphoto/Ray Lipscombe, Andy Potter; 71 Peter Gates; 72 IStockphoto, IStockphoto/Lukasz Kulicki; 74 IStockphoto/ Rich James; 75 Stanley Porter (rspb-images.com); 76 Peter Gates; 78 IStockphoto/Che Ballard; 79 IStockphoto/Maxim Filipchuk; 80 Simon Colmer and Abby Rex / Alamy; 81 IStockphoto/jim Pruitt; 82 Peter Gates; 83 Mark Boulton / Alamy; 84 IStockphoto/Andrew Howe; 85 Photoshot Holdings Ltd / Alamy; 86 IStockphoto/Chris Crafter; 88 IStockphoto/ Grant Shimmin, IStockphoto/Alan Tobey, IStockphoto/ Stephen Rees, IStockphoto/Andrew Howe, IStockphoto/Robert Blanchard; 89 IStockphoto/Alistair Forrester Shankie; 90 IStockphoto/Andy Gehrig, IStockphoto/Roger Whiteway; 91 IStockphoto/Heiko Grossmann, IStockphoto/Liz Leyden; 92 IStockphoto/Bruce Block; 93 IStockphoto/Denis Oregan; 94 Juniors Bildarchiv / Alamy, IStockphoto/Irina Shupletsova; 95 IStockphoto/Karel Broz; 96 IStockphoto/102 Ken Hewitt, IStockphoto/Andrew Howe, IStockphoto/Maurice van der Velden, blickwinkel / Alamy, Mark Hamblin (rspb-images. com), IStockphoto/Dieter Hawlan, Nigel Blake (rspb-images. com), Tomasz Sienicki; 97 Gerald Downey (rspb-images. com), Istockpphoto/Angela Oakes; 98 Natural Visions / Alamy, IStockphoto/Andrew Howe, IStockphoto/Andrew Howe, Mark Hamblin (rspb-images.com); 99 Mark Hamblin (rspb-images.com); 100 IStockphoto/Andrew Howe, Nigel Blake (rspb-images.com); 101 David Tipling (rspb-images. com); IStockphoto/102 Ken Hewitt, IStockphoto/Andrew Howe; 104 IStockphoto; 105 Andy Hay (rspb-images.com); 106 Shutterstock/Keith Naylor; 108 Phil McLean/FLPA, IStockphoto/Jon Meier; 109 Gerald Downey (rspb-images. com), Tomasz Sienicki; 110 IStockphoto/Dieter Hawlan, IStockphoto, IStockphoto/Robert Ellis; 111 IStockphoto, IStockphoto/Gary Martin, IStockphoto/Andrew Howe, Istockpphoto/Angela Oakes; 112 IStockphoto; 113 IStockphoto/ Lisa Valder, B. Borrell Casals/FLPA; 114 IStockphoto/Maurice van der Velden; 116 blickwinkel / Alamy; 118 IStockphoto, IStockphoto/Greg Nicholas, IStockphoto/Dmitry Maslov; 119 IStockphoto/Charles Schug; 120 IStockphoto/Murat M. Evirgen; 121 IStockphoto/Uli Hamacher; 122 IStockphoto/Nic Taylor. Illustrations throughout Peter Gates.